Self-Care for Clinicians in Training

Self-Care for Clinicians in Training

A Guide to Psychological Wellness for Graduate Students in Psychology

LEIGH A. CARTER AND
JEFFREY E. BARNETT

OXFORD
UNIVERSITY PRESS

OXFORD
UNIVERSITY PRESS

Oxford University Press is a department of the University of
Oxford. It furthers the University's objective of excellence in research,
scholarship, and education by publishing worldwide.

Oxford   New York
Auckland   Cape Town   Dar es Salaam   Hong Kong   Karachi
Kuala Lumpur   Madrid   Melbourne   Mexico City   Nairobi
New Delhi   Shanghai   Taipei   Toronto

With offices in
Argentina   Austria   Brazil   Chile   Czech Republic   France   Greece
Guatemala   Hungary   Italy   Japan   Poland   Portugal   Singapore
South Korea   Switzerland   Thailand   Turkey   Ukraine   Vietnam

Published in the United States of America by
Oxford University Press
198 Madison Avenue, New York, NY 10016

Library of Congress Cataloging-in-Publication Data
Carter, Leigh A.
Self-care for clinicians in training : a guide to psychological wellness for graduate students
in psychology / Leigh A. Carter and Jeffrey E. Barnett.
    pages cm
Includes bibliographical references and index.
ISBN 978–0–19–933535–0 (paperback)
1. Clinical psychology—Study and teaching (Graduate)   2. Clinical psychology—Study
and teaching (Internship)   3. Clinical psychologists—Training of—Psychological
aspects.   4. Medical students—Life skills guides.   5. Medical students—Mental
health.   6. Graduate students—Life skills guides.   7. Graduate students—Mental health.
I. Barnett, Jeffrey E.   II. Title.
RC467.7.C38 2014
616.890076—dc23
2014001793

9 8 7 6 5 4 3 2 1
Printed in the United States of America
on acid-free paper

To graduate students in psychology everywhere, who devote every day to learning and improving themselves to help others. LAC

To my many student collaborators over the years. Each has been a joy to work with and an important part of my overall wellness plan. JEB

Contents

Acknowledgments

The authors would like to extend their sincerest appreciation to Sarah Harrington, Andrea Zekus, Emily Perry, and the editorial staff at Oxford University Press for helping us turn an idea that started in an office several years ago into fruition, and for assisting us every step of the way in this process. We also express our thanks to our expert copy editor, Mary Anne Shahidi, and to our talented cover designer, Katrina Noble. We would also like to thank Deborah Haskins, PhD, and Heather Z. Lyons, PhD, for their thoughtful and helpful suggestions in earlier drafts of this book. Finally, we would like to extend our warmest appreciation to our colleagues and friends who volunteered to share their personal self-care lessons and activities throughout this book—Elizabeth Bailey, Sarah Brager, Melinda Capaldi, Rebecca Dean, Valerie Faure, Douglas Girard, Jon Gorman, Sylvia Hanna, Lindsay Klimik, Rachel Lawson, Jueta McCutchan, Arianna Perra, Margaret Perry, and Catherine Ruscitti.

Introduction

Congratulations! You have successfully navigated the very stressful graduate school application process and gained acceptance into a graduate program. You worked very hard in college to reach this point, spending countless hours studying, writing papers, doing clinical work and research, and then studying for the GRE, obtaining letters of recommendation, researching which programs to apply to, writing essays and completing applications, and then participating in interviews. It is your great work ethic, attention to detail, intellect, and perseverance that have helped you to achieve the important goal of acceptance into graduate school.

While this is a great accomplishment and the culmination of years of hard work, you now are at a new beginning. You have begun your training, and now find yourself on the path to becoming a future psychologist . . . so, now what? Successfully navigating your way through graduate school requires much more than completing the necessary coursework and clinical experiences. Whether today is your very first day of graduate school or you have been in a program for several years, you are likely already aware that as a graduate student in psychology you will make countless sacrifices and dedicate what may feel like a never-ending amount of time and energy (not to mention money!) in the pursuit of your professional training so that you will one day be able to assist others in need. You will devote much of yourself through your training to assist in the care and promote the wellness and effective functioning of those you treat.

Yet an irony often exists in the graduate school culture, such that many graduate students commit themselves to a field dedicated to the well-being of others while putting their own needs and well-being on hold, and at times overlooking them entirely. In fact, you will find that the qualities and abilities that helped you to be successful in college and gain admittance into graduate school will not be sufficient for success in graduate school in psychology. Writing excellent papers, studying for long hours, and receiving high grades on exams are not enough. Being a successful psychologist requires so much more than that, and many additional demands (personal, emotional, and interpersonal) will be placed on you throughout your professional training. On my (LC) very first day of graduate school, after receiving all the course syllabi, I called my family and half-jokingly told them that the next time they would see or hear from me would be in five years on my graduation day. This sense of both overwhelming demands and believing graduate school would now consume every minute of my life made any semblance of self-care seem foreign and impossible.

> *Many graduate students commit themselves to a field dedicated to the well-being of others while putting their own needs and well-being on hold.*

So, why then a book on self-care for graduate students when simply finding the time to read this book given your dozens of other demands and work commitments seems nearly impossible?

We can imagine asking a procrastinator to read a book on procrastination and being told months later that he was planning to read it . . . but just never got around to it. In a similar vein, we understand that giving a busy graduate student more to read and do may seem counterintuitive. Yet, consider the busy professional who never has time to have her automobile serviced because she is so busy driving to meetings and making money. One wonders how she will make time for her car breaking down and being without transportation for an extended period (plus the added expense of repairs and reduction of income due to loss of business). Similarly, we see taking the time to address our own self-care as an investment in ourselves and in our clients. We see it as a necessary part of our professional responsibilities and obligations.

The reality is that as a graduate student and future psychologist, you are still human and susceptible to life's many challenges. Furthermore, the experience of graduate school in psychology presents a unique set of challenges, demands, and stressors. In training, you are called upon to begin learning about and taking on the responsibility of assisting those in psychological distress. You also face countless additional stressors such as financial constraints, limited experience in your field of study or practice, navigation of the transition into graduate school, challenges with research projects, the internship process and experience, personal life challenges, as well as adjustment to and balance of professional and personal roles simultaneously.[1] Yet unlike other fields where tools or instruments are often used as the vehicle for change, in psychology *you* are the vehicle for change. Training in psychology also includes the uniquely challenging element of self-examination and introspection of your own psychological and emotional history and well-being. If these challenges and stressors are not adequately addressed, they may adversely affect you personally and professionally, undermining your clinical competence and having harmful consequences for the clients you are treating and trying to help.

This book was created to assist you in recognizing the challenges and stressors that come with the path you've chosen, and to begin practicing and incorporating a lifestyle of self-care. Through its use we hope you will learn and then consistently apply the attitudes and skills needed to promote your own ongoing wellness, helping to ensure competence now and throughout your career.

Self-care is the ongoing practice of self-awareness and self-regulation for the purpose of balancing psychological, physical, and spiritual needs of the individual.[2] It is a vital ingredient for preventing and repairing distress, problems with professional competence, burnout, and vicarious traumatization as psychologists. As noted, you are in many ways your own instrument in the work that you do and the care you provide to others, so if you don't take adequate ongoing care of yourself, your ability to help others may be reduced. The practice of self-care is simply not optional, nor a requirement

> *Self-care is the
> ongoing practice of
> self-awareness and
> self-regulation for the
> purpose of balancing
> psychological,
> physical, and
> spiritual needs.*

for a select few who are vulnerable or weak, but a necessary component in maintaining clinical competence and for providing ethical and competent care to clients. All mental health professionals, regardless of their particular circumstances,[3] have an obligation to practice self-care.

I'm Just a Grad Student. Why Start Now?

Self-care is a process that will require repeated adjustments and modifications in response to changes in your personal and professional lives—the self-care practices you establish now may not be the same as the ones you practice as a seasoned psychologist. But whatever your self-care routine, inadequate self-care at any stage of your professional journey, including graduate school, can have devastating effects for you, for those you care about in your personal life, and for those you serve professionally.

While a significant amount of research exists on the topic of self-care, much of it focuses on the circumstances and needs of practicing mental health professionals—not students—so the risk factors and sources of distress, vicarious traumatization, problems with professional competence, and burnout in this literature may be quite different from those faced by a graduate student. As a result, the literature on recommended self-care practices is often not entirely applicable to the graduate student's circumstances and needs. Furthermore, many graduate training programs do not adequately address the practice of self-care: In fact, 50% of graduates recently reported that their graduate programs did not promote self-care among students.[4] Given the stressors and challenges you will face during this phase of your professional development and training as well as in your personal life, it is essential that you develop relevant and appropriate self-care strategies to attend to present and anticipated future challenges.

Too often discussions of self-care and psychological wellness arise *after* problems with professional competence or symptoms of burnout have already been identified. Indeed, psychological wellness and self-care for mental health professionals continues to focus mainly on strategies and ideas as reparative measures. In contrast, this handbook aims to help shift our profession toward a prevention approach to self-care and psychological wellness. Utilizing self-care practices and identifying potential signs of and risk factors for distress, problems with professional competence, vicarious traumatization, and burnout as a means of prevention may serve as a powerful force for reducing the prevalence and severity of these difficulties and their impact on you. At the same time, observing self-care practices will enhance your quality of life, relationships, and health, and promote your clinical effectiveness.

Furthermore, it is during graduate school that your professional identity is significantly shaped and becomes established. Thus the attitudes, beliefs, and practices you develop as a graduate student will likely impact how you address these issues for years to come. This is another important reason that attention to self-care cannot wait. In short, all graduate students have a responsibility to begin developing lifestyles of self-care now, and to continually return to and make adjustments to these self-care lifestyles as new obstacles, challenges, and even opportunities present themselves throughout the course of their graduate and professional careers.

All graduate students have a responsibility to begin developing lifestyles of self-care now.

Throughout this book you will find the feature "Voice of Experience: One Psychologist's Perspective." In this feature, the second author (JB), an experienced practicing psychologist, educator, and supervisor, shares his personal reflections on the topics being addressed. These candid remarks will help illustrate how each of us is vulnerable to the effects of distress and how we must each actively work to promote our ongoing wellness through the use of self-care strategies at every phase of our career.

How to Use This Handbook

This handbook was created for all graduate students in psychology. While a particular emphasis is placed on graduate students in training to become clinicians, the book can be utilized by students in all fields of applied and research-based areas of psychology. As you

Voice of Experience: One Psychologist's Perspective

Even after over 30 years as a psychologist, I still need to actively work on self-care and balance. There is so much in the field of psychology that excites me, and there are so many aspects of the work that I enjoy and find rewarding. I often need to hold myself back from accepting every opportunity, whether it be serving on a committee in a professional association, accepting a colleague's offer to coauthor a journal article or book, accepting new referrals in my practice, and the like. Even today, I regularly struggle with setting limits and saying "no," working to maintain balance in my life. Whenever I lose track of this I find myself feeling increasingly stressed and those around me (in both my personal and professional lives) experience the effects of it—and let me know!

read, you will explore three important elements related to self-care and psychological wellness. Part I of the book will assist you with developing self-awareness and self-monitoring abilities regarding distress, problems with professional competence, burnout, and vicarious traumatization. Continuing on, in Part II you will find information and activities to assist you in developing your own personalized self-care plan. Finally, in Part III you will learn about ways to expand and apply self-care practices beyond yourself in order to assess and assist in establishing a culture of self-care in your own graduate program.

Every individual has unique sources of distress and distinctive risk factors that result in specific self-care needs. Thus it is important to keep in mind that while each chapter presents a variety of examples related to graduate students, self-care and psychological wellness are different for each individual. Throughout this book you are therefore encouraged to become actively engaged with the material and to reflect on how the information is specifically relevant to your own needs, personal and professional situations, and unique preferences.

Each chapter includes a case example to illustrate the point being made, not only to present representative challenges and difficulties, but also to highlight possibilities for effectively responding to them.

At the conclusion of each chapter you will find features such as checklists, informal assessments, and planning activities, as well as an ongoing reflection journal designed to help you increase awareness and insight into your own personal and professional relationship to self-care and psychological wellness, and to create realistic and practical action plans and strategies so that you can begin putting this knowledge into practice. The idea is for you to not only read about self-care and psychological wellness, but to actively work to infuse this material into your life, eventually coming to embody the principles taught in this handbook in your own unique and personal way.

As your personal and professional lives change over time, your self-care practices and attention to the potential challenges and stressors associated with your job must change as well, adapting as necessary to attend to your needs. As such, this handbook is intended as a resource for you to return to throughout your professional career. Each new phase of your career and your personal life will bring about new challenges that must be considered and addressed in a thoughtful manner. You can regularly return to this handbook for self-care tune-ups. This practice is consistent with the goal of prevention emphasized throughout this book. In doing so you can assess for signs or symptoms of problems with psychological well-functioning, making needed adjustments in your lifestyle. These may include making changes to better achieve balance in the face of changes in personal and professional demands, trying new time-management techniques as changes occur in your life, and continually adjusting your self-care lifestyle. These are just some ways this handbook may serve as a resource now and in the future.

One final thought for you as you prepare to embark on this journey of learning and attending to your self-care and psychological wellness: Self-care is a gradual process. It is unrealistic, overwhelming, and contrary to the promotion of healthy well-being to attempt to accomplish everything in this book or to achieve a certain specified degree of self-care and psychological wellness overnight. Self-care is not like a race to be won, and it is not an all-or-nothing phenomenon. Rather than thinking of crossing a self-care finish line, it is best to think of self-care

Think of self-care as a process and a lifestyle that you establish over time and that evolves over the course of your entire career. as a process and a lifestyle that you establish over time and that evolves over the course of your entire career. Beginning to make even the smallest of changes today as the first steps in your self-care journey can be an invaluable means of establishing a foundation for lifelong well-being.

We are delighted that you have chosen this handbook to assist you in beginning your self-care journey. We hope it will be an enriching and fulfilling one for you.

Part I

Beginning the Self-Care Journey

Tuning in and Assessing for Symptoms, Risk Factors, and Warning Signs

Exploring Your Sources
of Distress

Welcome to Graduate School

Zara graduated at the top of her class in college and spent two years working before enrolling in graduate school for psychology, and now she is adjusting to her new life. She misses her previous job that allowed her to leave her work at the office and relax at home in the evenings. Now, she finds herself having difficulty managing her time, often staying up until 1 or 2 a.m. many nights to complete her work, always feeling that there is more to do. With all the time Zara spends on her schoolwork, she is barely able to stay in touch with family and friends from home, who live over 400 miles away. Zara's partner, who lives in another state, has also become increasingly frustrated with her having so little time for him and always sounding tired when they talk on the phone. He does not understand why she continues to work well into the night most evenings. Zara has tried to talk with some of her classmates about this, but feels uncomfortable opening up to them since she doesn't yet know them very well. She wonders whether they will understand what she is going through and whether she is the only one struggling with managing graduate school.

Stress, stress, stress! Each and every one of us is likely all too familiar with it. It does not take extensive scientific theories to determine that graduate school will likely be, or already has been, a source of stress for you. Whether you have found yourself up late at night worrying, raiding the freezer for that tub of ice cream while studying for finals, or being curt on the phone with a friend after a long day, you likely have some idea of what stress looks like for you. But, like Zara's example, stress is often complex and comes from a variety of sources. Given the nature of stress, often the last thing you or anyone else would like to do is look more closely at it. Yet by better understanding your stress and exploring its causes and implications, you can begin to more healthfully manage it throughout graduate school.

What Is Distress?

Although it is unlikely that you will share the exact same difficulties as Zara, her experience is representative of many of the challenges faced by graduate students. It is impossible to be immune to the experience of stress, or even further what we refer to as *distress*, not only during graduate school but throughout the course of your professional and personal life.

> *Distress can be defined as "emotional reactions of the clinician in response to ongoing challenges, stressors, or demands in one's life."*

But what exactly is distress? For psychologists and those in training, distress can be defined as "emotional reactions of the clinician in response to ongoing challenges, stressors, or demands in one's life."[1] Distress is your subjective emotional response to these ubiquitous and ever-present circumstances.

All of us experience and carry with us some degree of distress on a daily basis. Distress is neither static nor episodic, but rather falls on a continuum and changes as your life changes. It may occur at a minimal level that you may not even be fully aware of, and to a certain extent can even be beneficial to your overall level of productivity, because in small and appropriate doses it can motivate you. Over time your level of distress can increase in response to situations such as an upcoming project or exam, the illness or death of a family member, a move to a new city, a client's attempted suicide, pressure to perform well in school and in your clinical work, and the like. The list of what can contribute to an increase in the level of distress you experience is endless. At the end of this chapter you will find a distress self-assessment designed to help you gauge the current levels of distress in both your personal and professional life.

Tuning In

Take a moment to recall a time when you recognized signs of distress in a classmate, friend, or family member. It may be easier to recognize signs of distress in others than in ourselves. Psychologists have been found to be no better at tuning in to their own stress than are non-psychologists, and in fact many struggle to accurately assess their own distress levels. Psychologists have also been found to experience significantly higher levels of emotional distress in contrast to their own self-perceptions and self-assessments of their distress levels.[2] In other words, we're often more stressed out than we realize!

Do you find yourself occasionally denying you are stressed and continuing to "work through it"? Or perhaps you bury your head under the pillow, hoping everything will pass over or magically work itself out? Just as you are in tune with your body when you start to feel sick, so too is it important to be in tune with your experience of distress. If you are not aware of the presence or extent of the distress you are feeling, or its likely consequences, you will certainly be less likely to take needed actions to address or remedy it.

As a graduate student preparing to enter the mental health field, you are likely to also struggle with accurately assessing your changing distress level over time. Additionally, some have suggested that graduate students have more difficulty than do practicing professionals with recognizing the signs of distress or correctly responding to their distress.[3] Considering the combination of the limited amount of professional training acquired thus far and the level of stress that graduate students experience, monitoring and assessing your level of distress can be a challenge.[4] Are you able to truly recognize within yourself when you are distressed, the level of this distress, and its impact on you? And once you do assess your level of distress, what do you do about it?

Voice of Experience: One Psychologist's Perspective

What are my sources of distress, and why is it so difficult to recognize them when they arise? Unless I make a conscious effort to be on the lookout for them, feelings of distress can creep up on me and take me by surprise. Fortunately, I have learned some lessons over the years: Seeing eight clients back-to-back without any breaks, regardless of the reason, just isn't a good idea; when I have a full schedule there is no time left for all the little things that can come up (returning phone calls, handling crises, etc.) and that always do; and when I take on too much at work I increasingly feel pressure from the "demands" in my personal life, even from things I've previously enjoyed, and my ability to effectively respond to them goes down dramatically.

What Is Your Distress Recipe? Understanding the Many Contributors to Distress

Although distress is a common experience among graduate students within the mental health professions, the sources of distress are unique to every individual. Distress is a melting pot of numerous personal and professional demands, challenges, and stressors; no two students share the exact same ingredients of their own distress; and ingredients will impact students in different ways. Therefore, as you attempt to increase awareness of your current experience of distress, it is important to consider and reflect on the many potential professional and personal sources of distress you may be facing. Throughout the remainder of this chapter, take time to consider the extent to which, if at all, each of the challenges and stressors discussed may be contributing to distress in your own life now, or may potentially contribute to distress in the future.

Professional Sources of Distress

Beginning graduate school	• Move to a new city
	• Distance from personal and professional support networks at former institution, former city

Academic and programmatic stressors	• Transition into graduate student role: adjusting out of undergraduate role; adjusting out of career/employment role
	• Coursework and studying
	• Comprehensive exams
	• Time management for meetings
	• Multiple roles and responsibilities as graduate student: student/clinician-in-training/client/researcher/teaching assistant/research assistant; simultaneously expert and trainee
	• Continuous evaluation, observation, and assessment of your performance
	• Multiple, ongoing, and strict deadlines
	• Management of updated or changing program requirements
	• Fear of dismissal when not meeting program standards—navigation of evaluation and review process
	• Limited cultural diversity, sensitivity, and/or respect in program or training
Interpersonal stressors	• Navigation of conflicting expectations and standards of professors and supervisors
	• Negative or unsupportive program environment (from faculty, administration, peers)
	• Relationships with classmates/cohort/lab mates
	• Negative or unsupportive relationship with advisor, supervisor, dissertation chair, principal investigator, and so forth
	• Navigation of self-disclosure with classmates, professors, supervisors, and clients
Stressors of research	• Match with a dissertation chair or principal investigator
	• Pressure for publication
	• Deadlines
	• Obstacles in research (IRB approval, finding participants, data collection, data analysis)
	• Ongoing editing of research/dissertation writing

Stressors of clinical work/ practicums/ internship	• Feelings of isolation in clinical work • Management of challenging patient behaviors: suicidality/violent clients/clients with chronic conditions • Securing of a clinical placement or externship • Internship—decision about where to apply: clinical/ training considerations; personal considerations (moving close to or away from partner/family, geographic limitations, etc.) • Application/interview/match process • Financial strain of application/interview process • Adjustment to internship—new placement, potential new city, leaving social supports again • Work-life balance on internship

Personal Sources of Distress

Financial	• Student loans and mounting debt • Limited opportunity and time for employment • Financial obligations (rent/mortgage, car, groceries, minor luxuries, supporting additional family members)
Personal relationships	• Multiple roles and responsibilities: partner/spouse/ child/sibling/parent/friend • Relationship difficulties (meeting people, marital difficulties, separation/divorce, problems with friends/ family members) • Attempts to establish relationships, dating, starting a family, raising children • Pressure to spend more time with loved ones in the face of academic and clinical responsibilities
Health and well-being	• Fatigue • Mental or physical health problems • Limited time and attention for exercise, eating well, adequate sleep • Caretaking of ill child or family member (time, emotional/financial support) • Pregnancy, fertility challenges, miscarriage, adoption process

Balancing	• Balancing time and demands of professional and personal responsibilities
	• Associated feelings of guilt when choosing one over the other
	• Limited time and attention to do it all
	• Consequences when personal/professional responsibility is not completed

Zara's Distress: Beginning Steps She Can Take Now

Zara's present sources of distress appear to primarily relate to her recent transition to graduate school. In her professional life, she is exhibiting distress in the areas of time management and navigating her workload. In her personal life, her poor sleep habits, limited communication with friends and family, and strain in her romantic relationship are sources of additional distress. Once Zara begins to identify her distress and where it is coming from, she can consider prioritizing her several areas of distress and choosing one or two to begin working on. Because many of Zara's current issues appear connected to her overall adjustment to graduate school, setting small goals such as prioritizing 8 hours of sleep per night, speaking with senior-level classmates to learn how they adjusted to the graduate program, and creating a schoolwork schedule can assist her in beginning to attend to her distress. Additionally, setting up daily or weekly scheduled phone or video-chat sessions with family, friends, and her partner may help Zara to manage maintaining her personal relationships as she navigates her graduate program.

Assess Your Distress

Rate each of the following professional and personal sources of distress for how distressing they are for you presently. Use a scale of 0–10, with 0 representing not distressing at all, and 10 representing among the most significant sources of distress for you.

PROFESSIONAL

Coursework _____

Dissertation/research work _____

Internship search and application process _____

Time management (coursework, meetings, jobs, etc.) _____

Fulfillment of clinical requirements _____

Practicum/externship search and application process _____

Student loans/financial constraints _____

Competition among classmates _____

Research or teaching assistant position _____

Recent evaluation of your academic or clinical work _____

Adjustment to a new location for graduate school _____

Work with a violent client _____

Limited clinical training and/or feelings of clinical incompetence _____

Client endorsing suicidality _____

Record keeping and documentation requirements for clinical work _____

Professional organization/association responsibilities _____

Return and/or adjustment to role as *graduate* student _____

Adjustment to the responsibilities, expectations, and environment of graduate program _____

Potential emotional isolation of clinical work _____

Challenges/conflicts in supervision _____

Cohort/peer relation problems _____

Demands of faculty and/or supervisors _____

Professional challenges related to personal diversity factors _____

PERSONAL

Romantic or marital difficulties _____

Fatigue _____

Guilt about not spending enough time with family/friends _____

Pregnancy (emotional, physical, financial) _____

Limited social outlets _____

Illness or death of family member or friend _____

Financial difficulties _____

Balancing role as a parent _____

Role as caretaker or provider for family member _____

Geographic separation from social support _____

Experience/management of personal mental or physical illness or disability _____

Difficulty staying in touch with friends or family members _____

Household chores or responsibilities (daily upkeep, bills, etc.) _____

Relational difficulties with parents, siblings, or other family members _____

Personal health _____

Marital separation/divorce _____

Relocation: looking for a new place to live, buying a home, and so forth _____

Personal life on hold during graduate school _____

Balance of additional jobs/work outside of school _____

Limited time to spend with romantic partner or spouse _____

Inadequate time for exercise and/or leisure time activities _____

Pressure from friends and/or family members to spend more time with them _____

Reflection Activity

Write three words that best describe how you feel when you are distressed.

Review the professional and personal sources of distress you endorsed in the previous checklist. What are the most significant factors contributing to the distress you are presently experiencing?

Describe and reflect on any similarities or common themes among the sources of distress you endorsed.

Based on the sources of distress you identified in the self-assessment checklist, develop a list prioritizing the different demands and sources of distress you are presently experiencing.

Recognizing and Addressing Problems with Professional Competence

When the Personal Becomes Professional

Peter is in his third year of graduate school. A few months ago his father was diagnosed with a terminal illness, so Peter has been spending his weekends traveling back and forth to his parents' home to spend time with his father. Yet he often feels guilty for not being able to spend more time with his dad, given all of the graduate school demands he is also trying to balance. His siblings have told him he is not "pulling his weight" in taking care of their father, but Peter feels this is unfair: Unlike the vacation days and sick leave his siblings enjoy in their jobs, graduate school offers no such benefits. He has also been having difficulty concentrating when working with clients, not only from being tired after staying up late to do the work he no longer has time for on the weekends, but also from thinking about his father while in sessions. He has become increasingly less empathic, at times even short tempered, and often appears irritated by his clients—particularly a new client whose presenting problem relates to bereavement issues. Peter has considered a leave of absence, but decided it would be better to just "push through," thinking the leave would create only more stress for himself and set him behind even further in his work.

Now that you are more familiar with distress and have identified signs of it in your own life, you have probably come to realize that it is nearly impossible for any of us to avoid at least some degree of distress at some point in time. But what happens, and how will you know, when your distress reaches more significant—and potentially harmful—levels?

Unfortunately, your body and mind are not triggered for alarms to automatically sound or warning signs to pop up when your distress levels rise. The onus is once again on you to be able to recognize and respond to problems.

Problems with Professional Competence

First and foremost, your own distress can no longer be ignored when it begins to impact the quality and effectiveness of your work. In such instances the concept of "problems with professional competence" must be considered.[1] Problems with professional competence for psychologists and those in training can be defined as "the interference in ability to practice psychotherapy, which may be sparked by a variety of factors and results in a decline in therapeutic effectiveness."[2] Professional competence expands beyond the practice of psychotherapy, though, so as a graduate student a decline in the quality of your academic, clinical, or any other professional work can be considered a sign of problems with professional competence.

Not every graduate student or psychologist will develop problems with professional competence, but we are all at risk. What puts one at risk for problems with professional competence? Typically, the transition from simply experiencing distress to the development of actual problems with professional competence occurs when individuals lack appropriate and effective means to address the stressors and challenges contributing to their distress.[3] In other words, it's not the fact that we are feeling distressed that is so potentially harmful, but how we deal with and manage that distress.

Psychologists who experience more stressors in work or life also experience more distress in work or personal life and problems with professional competence in their professional work.[4] Essentially, this all means that those who lack positive coping strategies to respond to their distress are at risk. This is why taking the time to regularly assess your distress levels and contributors to distress is key, as is having healthy and effective strategies to tend to your distress in efforts to reduce the risk of problems with professional competence (these strategies are discussed in Chapter 10).

Think of a small grease fire—a common enough occurrence in most household kitchens. Like distress, these fires can start off small and if properly attended to with a fire extinguisher the damage is often minimal. Once addressed you can easily move on with your life. But if you ignore the fire or lack appropriate, effective, and timely ways to notice and then respond to it, the consequences can be great, just as if you do not sufficiently attend to your individual experiences of distress. The consequences of problems with professional competence can be significant for you and those you treat.

Warning Signs of Problems with Professional Competence

How will you be able to tell that your professional competence may be at risk due to the distress you're experiencing?

- Incomplete or substandard documentation or clinical paperwork
- Fatigue or difficulty concentrating during class or psychotherapy sessions
- Arriving late or leaving early, before all the day's required responsibilities are completed
- Ongoing interpersonal difficulties with peers, colleagues, faculty, or supervisors
- Blurring or violating boundaries (e.g., sharing increasingly more about yourself with clients, increasing your use of touch with clients)
- Unprofessional or negligent practice (e.g., failing to make legally mandated reports, inappropriate relationships with clients)

Voice of Experience: One Psychologist's Perspective

We each have our individual warning signs that distress is moving us toward the point of diminished competence in our professional functioning. While it may be embarrassing to acknowledge, we all experience them. For me, some include the following: watching the clock during a session with a client and doing running calculations of how many minutes remain in the session, walking from my office to the waiting room and hoping that the next client will not show up, and finding the needs of those in my personal life to be a burden and wondering why they cannot be more supportive and understanding of me.

What Are the Chances that This Will Happen to You?

You may be thinking that you will not have to worry about problems with professional competence during your career, and we hope this will be true. Unfortunately, problems with professional competence are common in the field of psychology, and as a graduate student it is important to recognize your risk for experiencing these difficulties today and in the future.

- 74.3% of psychotherapists surveyed reported experiencing distress, and 36.7% reported that they believed their experience of distress negatively impacted the quality of care they provided to their clients (potential sign of problems with professional competence).[5]
- 85% of professionals endorsed the belief that it is unethical to work when distress is hindering one's ability to work effectively, yet nearly 60% admitted to doing it.[6]

As we have previously stated, problems with professional competence are not limited to seasoned professionals. Graduate students have also been identified as exhibiting signs of problems with professional competence.

- 72% of doctoral programs and 10% of internship sites identified trainees experiencing problems with professional competence.[7]
- 85% of graduate psychology students surveyed identified at least one peer with professional competence problems within his or her program.[8]

- Some of the most commonly reported issues impacting professional competence among graduate students include the following:
  - Personality disorder
  - Depressive symptoms
  - Adjustment disorder
  - Anxiety symptoms
  - Alcohol problems[9]

Tend to your professional competence on an ongoing basis, both with preventative actions and reparative measures when problems arise. If you are experiencing problems with professional competence, it is crucial that you understand the seriousness of this issue and seek the means to address it for the sake of your own well-being and of those with whom you work and interact. "Competence is seen as both a standard with minimal expectations and an aspirational ideal that one strives for on an ongoing basis."[10]

Building Competence 101

As we discuss this notion of problems with professional competence, it is also important to think about what competence really means for you as a graduate student in the field of psychology. Competence incorporates not only knowledge, skills, attitudes, and values, but also the ability to effectively utilize them.[11] Competence in a specific area, technique, or field therefore requires knowledge about that particular area of focus, skill in the specific practices involved, and the ability to demonstrate and apply those skills effectively.

Often for graduate students the focus of training is on knowledge and skills. You study and are tested on your knowledge and are asked to demonstrate your skill in mental health and research theories, practices, and a variety of other areas as a means of demonstrating developing competence. However, regardless of how much knowledge you may have or how often skills have been practiced, you cannot be considered competent if you are unable to effectively apply these skills. The ability to demonstrate effective competence is largely influenced by your emotional well-being as well as by the attitudes and values regarding self-care, psychological wellness, and quality of care you provide.[12] Competence really is the whole package!

The case example of Peter at the beginning of this chapter helps to demonstrate this concept of the three components of competence—knowledge, skills, and the ability to utilize them effectively. As an advanced-level graduate student, Peter has demonstrated high academic achievement and is quite knowledgeable when it comes to clinical theory and practice. He has also been involved in practicum training for three years now, and has therefore worked diligently at developing and practicing his clinical skills. However, the current stressors of his father's illness have begun to take their toll on him and the ability component of his competence. Peter's inability to concentrate during treatment sessions, his loss of empathy toward clients, and his falling behind in academic work inhibit him from demonstrating a proper level of competence despite his superior knowledge and skills.

It sounds enticing to think that perhaps after graduate school, or internship, or once settled into your professional career, competence can be checked off your to-do list as "achieved" and something you no longer have to worry about. Yet mental health professionals remain vulnerable to problems with professional competence indefinitely, so you must continually attend to competence throughout your career. This applies to areas of both professional competence and personal wellness. Addressing your psychological well-being is just as important as studying, conducting research, and engaging in direct training experiences.

Evaluating Your Competence

Self-Assessing and Monitoring

Assessing competence can begin with personal self-monitoring. At the end of this chapter is an exercise to assist you in thinking about your current level of competence and recognizing potential warning signs for problems. Begin by honestly reflecting on your areas of both strength and needed growth. Then, returning to the definition of competence (knowledge, skills, attitudes, and values, and the ability to implement them effectively), consider what contributes to your areas of needed growth. Do you require additional coursework or training to assist you? Or is this a problem with professional competence, in which heightened distress may be influencing your current competence level?

Self-monitoring is an important first step, but it alone is not sufficient! Often it can be difficult to assess competence solely based on your own personal thoughts and opinions— to some degree we all wear rose-colored glasses when evaluating ourselves. Consider how frequently we are able to identify a client's issues or difficulties before the client can. Or perhaps you can relate to the experience of being audio- or videotaped while conducting psychotherapy. You think it was a home run of a session, only to listen or watch it later, aghast and embarrassed by the missteps you made along the way. The point is it is much easier for others than it is for us to spot our own flaws and failures. Especially in times of distress it can be even more difficult to clear away the fog and recognize just how much you may be putting yourself or others at risk in the moment.

The Role of Training Programs and Evaluators

Training programs and evaluators can play an essential role in assisting you to assess your competence. Inquire about the systems and plans in place within your own program to get a feel for the level of attention it places on recognizing and assisting students experiencing such issues. Many programs offer regularly scheduled feedback sessions for students as part of their curricula. If such assistance is built in to your program, great! Take advantage of this help as much as possible.

All training programs have an ethical responsibility to address problems with professional competence[13] (see "The Ethical Imperative" section later in this chapter). This includes regularly assessing performance and providing feedback to graduate students,[14] thereby necessitating attention and response to signs of problems of professional competence a student may be exhibiting. Ask your evaluators to reflect on areas of strengths as well as possible warning signs they may have noticed. Regardless of whether or not warning signs exist, it is important that you develop methods to prevent problems with professional competence in the future.

Despite the ethical responsibility, many graduate programs fail to identify students who are at risk or struggling, and many do not have fortified intervention plans in place for students who may be exhibiting signs of problems with professional competence.[15] If your program has no such formal system in place, it is important that you proactively seek out assistance and feedback, particularly during times of heightened distress or concerns regarding your competence. This feedback and assistance can be solicited from faculty, supervisors, advisors, principal investigators in a lab, and anyone else who may evaluate you professionally. Take an active role and schedule feedback meetings with these individuals to discuss your competence. Not sure where to start? Here are some suggestions to help you when seeking feedback from faculty or other evaluators:

- "Hi Dr. S. I was wondering whether we could set up a time to meet soon. I would like to discuss my progress (in your class/with client X/this past semester in the graduate program) and think you could provide some insightful feedback for me. Is this something you think you can help me with and offer your perspective?"
- "As my supervisor, I appreciate the feedback you give me each week on specific areas of my clinical work where I am doing well. But I'm wondering whether we can take some time to reflect together on areas where I can improve. I would like to continue working on (processing/mindfulness techniques/etc.) and hope you can assist me with this. What are some of your thoughts?"

The Role of Peers

Quite often the people you spend the most time with during graduate school, your peers, may also be able to provide quality feedback on your level of competence, particularly regarding the ability aspect of competence. Be thoughtful about the peers you consult when seeking feedback—your best friend in the program may give you rave reviews, but will he or she be able to provide accurate and unbiased feedback? Highly competitive classmates may also be less than ideal candidates when seeking respectful and unbiased feedback. Seek peers who are knowledgeable or trained in the area of competence you need feedback on, who have worked with you or observed you in this area, and peers whom you trust. For example, if you receive group supervision, these peers may serve as a valuable and reliable resource. Keep in mind that asking for feedback from peers requires an element of humility and disclosure on your part, and thus may not be right for everyone. However, when sought out and received effectively, it can be highly rewarding and helpful.

Here are some sample conversation starters to help get you going when you are seeking peer feedback:

- "I know we don't usually talk about this in our program, but lately I've been really struggling with this one client. I leave each session and feel so lost. Do you know what I mean? I've never dealt with a client with suicidal ideation before, and to be honest, it makes me somewhat anxious . . . Has anyone else in the group ever felt this way? . . . What would it be like if next week in group supervision I brought in a clip of my recording and ask you all for some feedback?"
- "Hi, Sandy. I'm presenting my research in a few weeks at a conference. I know you have done some presentations before on a similar topic, and I was wondering whether you wouldn't mind letting me practice the presentation in front of you? I would really appreciate your honest feedback both on the content I am delivering and my presentation skills."

Peer monitoring is not only helpful, but an ethical necessity when it comes to professional competence. As a graduate student you are ethically bound not only to monitor your own ethical behavior and professional competence, but also to monitor the ethical conduct and functioning (including competence) of your colleagues and peers.[16] (For more on this, see Chapter 11.)

The Ethical Imperative

As a graduate student you are committed to upholding your profession's standards of ethics. How you work to prevent, address, and manage distress, problems with professional competence, burnout, and vicarious traumatization (see Chapters 3 and 4) has significant ethical implications. The Ethical Principles of Psychologists and Code of Conduct (APA Ethics Code) specifically addresses the responsibility of psychologists and graduate students in the areas of self-care and professional competence for oneself and among colleagues.[17] The following is a list of several aspirational principles and enforceable standards from the APA Ethics Code highlighting the ethical imperative of tending to problems with professional competence among individuals, training environments, and colleagues to promote our wellness and to prevent harm to those we serve.

Ethical Standards on Competence: Self Responsibilities

- Principle A: Beneficence and Nonmaleficence, states, "Psychologists strive to be aware of the possible effect of their own physical and mental health on their ability to help those with whom they work."[18]
- Ethical Standard 2.06, Personal Problems and Conflicts:
  (a) Psychologists refrain from initiating an activity when they know or should know that there is a substantial likelihood that their personal problems will prevent them from performing their work-related activities in a competent manner.
  (b) When psychologists become aware of personal problems that may interfere with their performing work-related duties adequately, they take appropriate measures, such as obtaining professional consultation or assistance, and determine whether they should limit, suspend, or terminate their work-related duties.[19]
- Standard 2.03, Maintaining Competence, states, "Psychologists undertake ongoing efforts to develop and maintain their competence."[20]
- Standard 3.04, Avoiding Harm, states, "Psychologists take reasonable steps to avoid harming their clients/patients, students, supervisees, research participants, organizational clients, and others with whom they work, and to minimize harm where it is foreseeable and unavoidable."[21]

Ethical Standards on Competence: Training Programs and Evaluators

- Standard 7.06, Assessing Student and Supervisee Performance, mandates psychologists in academic and supervisory roles to assess and provide feedback to trainees regarding their performance based "on relevant and established program requirements."[22]

Ethical Standards on Competence: Peer/Colleague Monitoring

- Standard 1.05, Reporting Ethical Violations, mandates that ethical violations be reported to the appropriate boards or committees.[23]

- Standard 1.04, Informal Resolution of Ethical Violations & Standard 1.05, Reporting Ethical Violations, mandates that concerns and issues related to peer or colleague competence first be addressed directly with colleagues and then if necessary "take further action appropriate to the situation."[24]

Bringing It Back to Self-Care . . .

These ethical standards emphasize your personal responsibility to maintain, monitor, and, if necessary, repair your own well-functioning. Personal and professional well-functioning have important implications for the ethical nature of your work, including the potential impact on those you treat clinically. These ethical standards also highlight the importance of continual self-care practices and the ongoing promotion of psychological wellness throughout your professional career.

What Can Peter Do?

In Peter's case, it is important for him to become aware of the potential impact of the emotional and practical aspects of his father's illness on his personal and professional well-being and functioning. In keeping with the ethical standards of the profession,[25] rather than ignoring his warning signs or simply trying to work through them, Peter should begin addressing the impact of his distress on himself and others, and actively seek consultation with trusted colleagues or supervisors. While he may feel embarrassed or fear punitive action from his program's administration if he brings this up to them, it is essential for him to recognize the risks of not seeking assistance for himself and in his professional work. With these colleagues or supervisors, Peter can develop a plan to help him better cope with this difficult situation and to decide whether and how he should limit his clinical responsibilities during this very challenging time. Examples of ways to respond include cutting back on his caseload, participating in personal psychotherapy, more actively utilizing his supervisor and colleagues for support, and if needed, taking a leave of absence from school.

Competence Self-Evaluation

Answer the following questions to help you evaluate your areas of competence and potential at-risk or problem areas. As a self-evaluation, be mindful of the limitations given your personal biases as you complete this.

1. List areas of knowledge and skill where you feel you are competent:

2. List attitudes and values you have that promote your competence and ability to demonstrate this knowledge and these skills effectively:

3. List ongoing stressors and difficulties you are experiencing in your professional life:

4. List ongoing stressors and difficulties you are experiencing in your personal life:

5. List any warning signs of problems with professional competence that might be present:

6. Write out resources you can access to assist you in assessing any risk factors or current problems with professional competence you may be vulnerable to:

Are You at Risk for Burnout?

When It's More than "Just a Little Stress"

The process of applying to internship and working on data collection for his dissertation has added significant demands to an already busy graduate schedule for Juan. Over the last three months he has felt increasingly tired and irritable, but presumes that this is to be expected given the stressful nature of dissertations and the internship application and selection process. Juan has also been completing an externship at a local state hospital, and his supervisor recently called him in for a meeting to discuss his progress. Juan's supervisor noted that Juan frequently arrives late, leaves early, or simply doesn't show up. In the meeting, Juan confessed to feeling that no matter how hard he works, his clients do not seem to show any signs of improvement: Juan referred to some clients' "laziness" and noted that he lacked confidence in his clinical skills and had an overall "why bother?" attitude. Juan's fiancée has also felt that Juan has been more tired and irritable recently, noticing that although Juan used to come home sharing what he learned that day at his training site, he now almost always comes home in a bad mood. When she has tried to address the changes that she has noticed with him, Juan typically responds by saying, "It's just a little stress," and that things will improve once his dissertation is completed and he matches for internship.

Isn't It Too Early for Burnout?

Burnout for graduate students? This may sound ironic or impossible when you consider that graduate students are just starting out in the field. It is all too easy, at the early stages of your career, to think of burnout as something you will "worry about" at a later time. This is because the term *burnout* in our profession is most often associated with the image of a seasoned psychologist, having worked for many years in the field, perhaps burned-out from working excessive hours, buried under mounting paperwork, and feeling emotionally depleted from treating challenging clients.

The reality is that the serious nature of burnout demands attention from psychologists at all career stages, including those in training. Just because you are not a seasoned veteran does not make you immune to burnout, and graduate students are also at risk. In fact, older clinicians have reported lower levels of burnout than have younger clinicians.[1] Furthermore, while not all psychologists and graduate students experience burnout, all are candidates for burnout,[2] with 60% of practicing psychologists having self-reported experiencing burnout over the course of their careers.[3] Establishing good habits and practices now that you can implement to prevent and address issues later on in your career, including burnout, can have a significant impact on the overall trajectory of your psychological wellness.

What Is Burnout?

Burnout is much more than just being tired or overworked. Thinking back to distress, burnout is "the terminal phase of therapist distress"[4]—the end result of distress that has not been attended to or addressed adequately. For many people the development of burnout is a gradual process that builds with time.[5] In fact, 88% of psychologists surveyed reported burnout rates in the low range, 8% in the moderate range, and 4% in the high burnout range,[6] suggesting that burnout can be experienced along a continuum. Immediately attending to low or moderate levels of burnout symptoms can help to prevent a progression into a more severe range of burnout and the much more significant and damaging professional and personal consequences that occur as a result.

Burnout is "the terminal phase of therapist distress."

Burnout Signs and Symptoms

While burnout can vary in appearance from one graduate student to the next, the three defining elements of burnout include emotional exhaustion, depersonalization, and decreased sense of accomplishment.[7]

- Emotional exhaustion
  - Feelings of emotional depletion
  - Inability to provide the emotional aspects of clinical work
- Depersonalization
  - Negative or callous attitudes regarding clients
  - Loss of empathic capabilities
- Decreased sense of accomplishment
  - Negative attitudes about self and professional accomplishments
  - Reduced sense of satisfaction and fulfillment in your work[8]
- Personal distress symptoms
  - For example, fatigue, insomnia, physical exhaustion, weight loss, irritability, boredom, excessive risk taking, increased substance use, family and relationship difficulties[9]
- Engagement in substandard practices of client care[10]

The truth is, like most graduate students you are likely to experience at one time or another some degree of emotional exhaustion, depersonalization, and/or decreased sense of accomplishment. Let's face it: Graduate school is hard, stressful, and demanding! For example, at this early stage of your professional career, having not yet accumulated decades of experience, you may be prone to negative feelings regarding your degree of accomplishments.

While it is natural for all of us to face each of the three individual components of burnout to some degree at different phases of our careers, experiencing all three components simultaneously and to a sizeable degree can have serious consequences. Note that you need not have problems with all three criteria for burnout (emotional exhaustion, depersonalization, decreased sense of personal accomplishment) to be experiencing burnout. Many psychologists and those in training, for instance, are at risk for the emotional exhaustion component of burnout, while most do not experience complete burnout in all three areas.[11] Assuming that your burnout symptoms can be ignored, or that they are less serious because you are not exhibiting symptoms in all three burnout categories, can be considerably risky because symptoms can spread and grow if not proactively addressed.

Risk Factors Contributing to Burnout

While you will never be entirely immune to burnout during graduate school or your professional career, several professional risk factors can increase your vulnerability to it. Learning about these risk factors is an important key to prevention. The following is a brief summary of the research on risk factors for burnout.

Workplace Setting

The setting in which you work can have a significant impact on your risk for professional burnout.

- Those in independent practice have reported lower levels of burnout than those in agency settings.[12]
- Psychotherapists in private practice settings reported among the lowest levels of burnout, with those in hospitals and public agencies reporting among the highest levels.[13]
- Commonly identified workplace risk factors for burnout include the following:
  - Experiencing feelings of not having much control over work activities
  - Working longer hours
  - Spending a significant amount of time on administrative or paperwork-related tasks
  - Working with fewer direct-pay clients.[14]
- Female psychotherapists in agency settings appear at greater risk for emotional exhaustion, while male psychotherapists appear at greater risk for emotional exhaustion in group independent practice settings.[15]

Questions to consider: What are the challenges, demands, and stresses associated with working in the settings where you are receiving your training? As a graduate student, do you have limited input and control over such factors as your caseload, schedule, administrative requirements, and lack of monetary compensation? To what extent might this lack of control serve as a potential risk factor for burnout?"

Managed Care

The practices and responsibilities involved with managed care can also impact your risk of burnout.

- Among independent practice psychotherapists, those surveyed reported that their highest source of stress was related to managed care.[16]
- Potential risk factors for burnout associated with managed care may include the following:
  ○ External limitations on services
  ○ Excessive amounts of paperwork
  ○ Additional time and cost to obtain reimbursement
  ○ Low reimbursement rates.[17]
- Psychotherapists more heavily involved in managed care caseloads (80% or more of caseload) reported higher levels of emotional exhaustion.[18]

Questions to consider: What is your involvement with managed care work at current or future training sites? How might the challenges of working within the managed care system impact your level of stress and feelings of control?

Client Population

The size and clinical characteristics of your caseload can also contribute to your risk of burnout.

- Negative client behaviors (e.g., suicidal, threatening, or dangerous) can serve as a risk factor for burnout, notably emotional exhaustion and depersonalization.[19]
- Psychotherapists who identified having larger caseloads than desired reported higher levels of burnout.[20]
- Commonly identified characteristics of stressful clients among psychotherapists include the following:
  ○ Borderline personality disorder
  ○ Depression

- ◦ Suicidality
- ◦ Psychotic symptoms
- ◦ Passivity
- ◦ Substance abuse
- ◦ Sociopathic behavior
- ◦ Acting out
- ◦ Physical violence.[21]

Questions to consider: What is your degree of control over and input into the makeup of your caseload, both in size and in client characteristics?

The Implications of Burnout

Your personal time and relationships are likely very valuable to you. None of us lives in a vacuum, and problems in our professional lives can flow into and influence our personal lives—and vice versa—and the experience of burnout is no exception.[22] Fatigue, cynicism, boredom, a depleted sense of your accomplishments, and other symptoms of burnout are likely difficult to leave at the office every day. Instead, you are likely to carry these symptoms with you into your personal life and relationships in a variety of ways, including (but not limited to) being emotionally withdrawn, having limited patience, and feeling fatigued.[23] It follows that the quality of your personal relationships will suffer as a result of professional burnout.

When the risk factors and symptoms of burnout are ignored or improperly addressed, there may be grave implications for your professional life and particularly for your clients. As professionals in mental health, we are in many ways our own instruments for change in the treatment we provide to others.[24] Not surprisingly, a correlation exists between psychotherapists' burnout and clients' perceptions of psychotherapists' effectiveness, their satisfaction with the therapeutic relationship, and their feelings regarding the overall success of the psychotherapy experience.[25] Burnout may also make psychotherapists, including graduate student clinicians, more susceptible to professional errors, which can certainly negatively impact clients. In the medical profession, advanced trainees who experienced higher levels of burnout and fatigue were more likely to report having committed at least one medical error.[26] The prevention of burnout is therefore essential not only in your professional role as a graduate student, but also as it relates to your academic life, your personal life, and your clients.

Stress or Burnout for Juan?

Remember our case example? Juan is currently experiencing stress in a number of academic and clinical areas. Like many other graduate students, he is trying to balance applying to internship, completing his dissertation, and meeting his current academic and clinical demands. However, the stress he is experiencing appears to be currently impacting him, his clients, and personal life in a significant and intense way, possibly suggesting burnout. Returning home from externship most evenings feeling more tired and irritable than usual, and expressing a negative attitude about his work experiences, suggest that Juan is experiencing *emotional exhaustion*. In addition, his impatient and negative attitudes toward clients could signal *depersonalization*. Finally, Juan appears to exhibit signs of a *decreased sense of personal accomplishment*, feeling overworked and ineffective in his clinical work.

Are You at Risk for Burnout?

The following is an exercise to help you monitor your potential risk factors and symptoms of burnout. Mark off all that currently apply to you.

PART I: RISK FACTORS

_____ Placement in hospital, prison, or community mental health setting

_____ Limited control over one's work activities

_____ Longer hours of work than usual

_____ Significant time spent on administrative tasks or paperwork

_____ A challenging client caseload (e.g., suicidal, violent, or threatening clients; clients that do not improve)

_____ Limited control over one's caseload

_____ Work with managed care

PART II: SYMPTOMS

_____ Fatigue

_____ Weight loss

_____ Increased irritability

_____ Boredom/distraction in sessions

_____ Excessive risk-taking

_____ Decreased sense of empathy toward clients

_____ Negative attitudes regarding clients

_____ Negative attitudes about yourself

_____ Feelings of a diminished sense of professional accomplishments

_____ Decreased satisfaction and fulfillment in school or clinical work

After completing the burnout exercise, rate your current level of each of the three factors of burnout.

1. EMOTIONAL EXHAUSTION

Remember that emotional exhaustion relates to feeling emotionally depleted and/or experiencing diminished ability to provide an adequate degree of the emotional elements of clinical work.

To what degree is your level of emotional exhaustion impacting the following areas?

Academically:

Low   Moderate   High

Clinical work:

Low   Moderate   High

Professional/administrative work:

Low   Moderate   High

Personal life:

Low   Moderate   High

2. DEPERSONALIZATION

Remember that depersonalization relates to developing negative or callous attitudes toward clients and loss of therapeutic empathy.

To what degree is your level of depersonalization impacting the following areas?

Academically:

Low   Moderate   High

Clinical work:

Low   Moderate   High

Professional/administrative work:

Low   Moderate   High

Personal life:

Low   Moderate   High

3. DECREASED SENSE OF PERSONAL ACCOMPLISHMENT

Remember that this relates to a diminished ability to recognize accomplishments in work and/or loss of satisfaction, interest, or fulfillment in your work.

To what degree is your level of decreased sense of personal accomplishment impacting the following areas?

Academically:

Low   Moderate   High

Clinical work:

Low   Moderate   High

Professional/administrative work:

Low   Moderate   High

Personal life:

Low   Moderate   High

Reflection Activity

As a graduate student, you must begin developing strategies right away in order to reduce your risk for burnout today and into the future.

Consider your own burnout risk factors. What are they?

In what ways can you begin to address them (e.g., in the areas of work setting and environment, managed care, and caseload)?

Risks of Clinical Work with Trauma

Beyond Empathy: When Feeling for Our
Clients Impacts Our Own Well-Being

Chloe is training at a local community mental health center. She has been at this site approximately six months and has enjoyed working with her clients, treating individuals mostly of mild to moderate impairment. Recently, Chloe began working with a new client who presented with a history of sexual abuse and trauma. Although receiving close supervision regarding this case, over the last month Chloe has found herself often thinking about this client, more so than her other clients. Despite making conscious efforts to avoid doing so, she finds herself imagining scenes from what her client has shared in sessions regarding the client's history of abuse, often times while in class or when trying to fall asleep at night. As a result, Chloe has felt excessively fatigued these past few weeks and has had difficulty concentrating in class. At times she experiences feelings of sadness and guilt about her client's experience. Given these reactions, she has begun to wonder whether she is "strong enough" to make it as a psychologist. She questions whether she will be able to handle clients with more severe pathology or traumatic histories, believing she should be able to leave these thoughts and feelings at the door of the treatment room and not carry them around with her.

What Are Vicarious Traumatization and Secondary Traumatic Stress?

At any level of your professional career and development, it is impossible to wholly check your personal life and history at the door when you enter a treatment room. In part, this is what contributes to your own unique and individual style and approach as a professional in psychology. It is also impossible to completely leave behind everything your clients have shared with you as you walk out of the treatment room at the end of the day. There are many things that your clients can share, discuss, or do that can impact your psychological wellness. If you have ever worried about a potentially suicidal or high-risk client over a long weekend, you have experienced firsthand the inability to completely "turn off" your professional side when outside the office or training site.

This is also the case when working with clients with traumatic histories. Regardless of the clinical niche you choose or areas of specialization you may develop over time, at some point in your career you are likely to find yourself working with at least one, and likely many, clients with histories of trauma. Even when trauma-related issues are not among the client's stated presenting problems, the client may have suffered trauma and abuse in the past. You may even have a particular interest in this area of psychology and like many others find it particularly rewarding work. Whether working with one or 20 clients with a trauma history, it can be particularly difficult to prevent this work from impacting you in your interactions with other clients, or in your personal life outside of the office.

Working with trauma clients can put you at risk for experiencing symptoms of vicarious traumatization and secondary traumatic stress.

With so many challenging clinical situations and populations, why does working with trauma clients get so much emphasis in a book on psychological wellness? Because working with trauma clients can put you at risk for experiencing symptoms of vicarious traumatization and secondary traumatic stress.[1] These can associatively contribute to distress, problems with professional competence, or even burnout, and in turn can influence your clinical abilities and negatively impact all of your clients.[2]

While the terms *vicarious traumatization* and *secondary traumatic stress* are often used interchangeably, vicarious traumatization specifically refers to the emotional and cognitive symptoms you may experience as a provider working with trauma victims,[3] while secondary traumatic stress involves behavioral symptoms that may occur when working with trauma populations.[4] These symptoms often result in response to histories of traumatic events experienced and shared by your clients and are "a natural byproduct of working with traumatized people."[5]

Voice of Experience: One Psychologist's Perspective

I remember early in my career treating a client who was referred for symptoms of depression. Going into this, I felt confident in my ability to help. Yet, as treatment progressed and my client shared her history of significant emotional, physical, and sexual abuse over an extended period of time, I found that I was ill-prepared for this experience. I was impacted by what she shared in ways I had not anticipated. I found myself thinking about and visualizing these experiences of abuse at other times of the day. I even noticed that I seemed more emotionally reactive with other clients, at times feeling angry and frustrated in response to their descriptions of difficulties they had experienced. Noticing myself becoming angrier in general and more preoccupied with my client's trauma, and feeling confused about and concerned by these reactions, I sought out consultation with a trusted colleague and entered ongoing clinical supervision to help better understand and address these issues and my reactions to them.

Risks, Warning Signs, and Implications

Although considered relatively normal reactions, vicarious traumatization and secondary traumatic stress can have significant negative implications for your professional and personal functioning. These can range from slight increases in distress to significant problems with professional competence or other consequences in your professional and personal life.

Secondary traumatic stress and vicarious traumatization may include posttraumatic stress disorder–like symptoms such as recollections, dreams, other imagery, and/or preoccupation about the client's traumatic event; avoidant behaviors such as making efforts not to think about or to avoid reminders of the client's trauma; loss of interest in certain activities; and hyperarousal such as difficulty sleeping or concentrating,[6] all of which can contribute to your levels of distress and/or problems with professional competence. Feelings of hopelessness, confusion, and increased isolation from one's support network, as well as numbness, cynicism, and emotional distance from clients have also been suggested as possible symptoms for the clinician.[7]

These symptoms can also negatively influence your personal life and relationships, lead to difficulties with following through on commitments or responsibilities, and increase levels of fatigue. Note that this is not a comprehensive list; there are countless ways in which the experience of vicarious traumatization can infiltrate your life.

Symptoms of Vicarious Traumatization and Secondary Traumatic Stress

---

- Experience of recollections or dreams about a client's traumatic event
- Preoccupation with a client's traumatic event
- Avoidance of reminders of a client's trauma
- Loss of interest in previously pleasurable activities
- Hyperarousal (e.g., difficulty sleeping, difficulty concentrating)
- Avoidance of clients
- Feelings of helplessness or confusion
- Increased sense of isolation from support networks
- Emotional numbing
- Cynicism

No two individuals will experience vicarious traumatization or secondary traumatic stress in the exact same way. This means that these symptoms will impact different areas of your professional and personal lives in different ways compared to other graduate students, so it is important that you maintain active awareness and self-monitoring for the presence of potential risk factors and signs of vicarious traumatization and secondary traumatic stress. Do not wait until you think you are "worse" than another peer or colleague, or until you experience *all* the symptoms.

Like the other components of psychological wellness we have discussed thus far, prevention and reparation of vicarious traumatization and secondary traumatic stress not only must focus on you, but must also consider the implications on your clinical work and the well-being of your clients—and not just the traumatized client in question, but all of those you treat. All of your clients can be influenced by you indirectly if, say, you are feeling fatigued in your work or are having difficulty concentrating. Or you may influence your clients in more direct ways: for instance, by feeling a need to provide more attention to the traumatized client at the expense of other clients. Ultimately, it is very important to recognize that your state of distress can inhibit the quality of care that you provide to the victimized client and to your other clients.[8]

It is very important to recognize that your state of distress can inhibit the quality of care that you provide to the victimized client and to your other clients.

When Our Own History Plays a Role

Your own unique background plays an important role in your work with trauma clients. While a personal history of trauma may be a source of empathy for you with clients who share traumatic histories, and thus serve to enrich the therapeutic relationship, this can also contribute to professional blind spots and the development of symptoms of vicarious traumatization and secondary traumatic stress. How does this work? While it varies for every individual, largely it has to do with the interaction between your client's traumatic history and emotional distress and related content in your own personal life or history—particularly "unresolved trauma."[9] Potential blind spots include overidentifying with a client whose traumatic history is similar to yours, or ignoring or encouraging unhealthy practices in the client.[10] Additionally, if you have a trauma history, working with trauma clients may trigger your own trauma history and result in the experience of the cognitive, emotional, or behavioral symptoms that define vicarious traumatization and secondary traumatic stress.

Psychologists, particularly women, have significant rates of past trauma in comparison to professionals in other fields, having reported high rates of traumatizing or stressful personal experiences (e.g., physical and sexual abuse, parental alcoholism, hospitalization of a parent with mental illness, parent or sibling death) that may result in greater risk of distress or problems with professional competence.[11] In fact, a history of childhood physical or sexual abuse was found among 69.93% of female psychologists and 32.85% of male psychologists,[12] highlighting the likelihood that many who enter the profession of psychology may be at increased risk for vicarious traumatization and secondary trauma.

Many successful and effective professionals choose careers in psychology in part in order to resolve their own histories of trauma, while others may be driven to the profession as a result of their history of fulfilling the caretaker role within their families, making work as a psychologist seem like the natural career choice.[13] This may be due to their familiarity with the caretaker role, an ability to identify with the experiences of certain clients, the fact that they may view a career in mental health as an opportunity to explore and attend to their own histories, or the "mastery of chaotic environments" gained as a result of such previous histories and experiences.[14] Take some time to consider for yourself your own personal motivations for entering this field. The reflection activity at the end of this chapter can be used to assist you in this.

All of this does not mean, however, that you must have a traumatic history in order to experience vicarious traumatization or symptoms of secondary traumatic stress or that you are immune to vicarious traumatization if you do not have a trauma history. Like the case example of Chloe, it is possible to be distressed and negatively impacted by the experiences of your clients without having shared a similar past.

The Graduate Student Risk

At this moment in your career, you are especially at risk for experiencing vicarious traumatization and secondary traumatic stress, particularly given your lack of experience working in the field.[15] Consider that professionals who worked with victims of trauma in their caseloads, who self-identified as having a personal history of trauma, and who had less than two years of professional experience demonstrate more problems in psychological well-being and elevated levels of distress than those with more years of experience.[16] Many psychologists report that their graduate training did not provide them with sufficient skills and knowledge for working with trauma clients in general, and in particular, with child abuse trauma.[17] Therefore, you may be among many of today's graduate students who feel ill-prepared not only to work with such clients, but also to recognize within yourself the early symptoms of vicarious traumatization or secondary traumatic stress and to attend to the potential consequences that working with these clients can have on your own psychological well-being. Mix in the prevalence of professionals with preexisting traumatic histories, and it becomes evident that it is crucial for you and all graduate students to be aware of your risk for vicarious traumatization and secondary traumatic stress.

I'm Working with a Trauma Client—Now What?

For clinicians working with trauma, you need to continuously assess yourself and ask, "How am I doing?"[18] Whether this is your first or fiftieth client with a history of trauma, such self-assessment can begin by considering your level of experience working with such clients and what you may need in terms of extra support to help you with this work (e.g., additional supervision time, entering a group supervision). Similarly, with many of the other threats to psychological well-functioning (distress, problems with professional competence, and burnout), your primary goal should be preventing vicarious traumatization and secondary traumatic stress symptoms, rather than waiting to address these issues after they arise.

Your primary goal should be preventing vicarious traumatization and secondary traumatic stress symptoms, rather than waiting to address these issues after they arise.

The tips that follow will help you to prevent symptoms of vicarious traumatization and secondary traumatic stress in yourself.

Tip #1: Get to Know Yourself

Self-monitoring is an important tool when it comes to preventing secondary traumatic stress and vicarious traumatization,[19] and becoming aware of your blind spots plays a significant role. No one psychotherapist can work effectively with all types of clients. Take time to reflect on your personal history, family history, and current challenges or issues. Are there aspects of your personal life that feel unresolved and that may make it difficult to work with clients who share similar histories or issues? It is important for everyone, and especially those with a history of trauma, to recognize the types of clients or clinical issues that may be challenging to work with. It is also essential to your own personal and professional well-being to consider taking time to attend and appropriately take care of those issues in your own life.

Getting to know yourself also means looking out for and recognizing times when clinical work, particularly with trauma clients, has opened vulnerabilities or triggers within yourself, manifesting in the cognitive, emotional, and behavioral symptoms of vicarious traumatization and secondary traumatic stress. Regularly conduct self-assessments of warning signs and symptoms of vicarious traumatization and secondary traumatic stress, and consider reviewing these assessments in supervision. (See "Checklist and Reflection Activity" at the end of this chapter to help you get started.)

Tip #2: Supervision

When working with a client with a trauma history, it is crucial that you engage in ongoing conversations with your supervisor to assist you in looking out for or addressing symptoms of secondary traumatic stress. Do not wait for your supervisor to initiate such conversations, especially if you already think you may be experiencing difficulties. Remember, ignoring these signs can have significant negative implications for you and your clients. It is important to openly discuss your emotional reactions to clients and how they may be impacting you. Merely focusing on diagnoses and treatment techniques, to the exclusion of your personal reactions, may be doing both you and your clients a disservice. Additionally, graduate students often have not developed the ability to decide whether or not they would like to and will work with a particular client. Have a discussion with your supervisor about what types of clients and clinical issues you anticipate will be the most challenging for you to work with, as a preventive measure against vicarious traumatization and secondary traumatic stress.

Tip #3: Personal Psychotherapy

You may consider engaging in personal psychotherapy (see Chapter 8) and using these sessions to address thoughts or feelings regarding the process of treating a client with a trauma history.[20] It also can be a vital tool to assist you with Tip #1, as personal psychotherapy can help you identify, explore, and work on personal histories, present personal issues, or vulnerabilities in clinical work. If you have a history of trauma, you should consider utilizing psychotherapy as a self-care practice to discuss and address any unresolved conflicts from your past. This can help to reduce the risk of vicarious traumatization and secondary traumatic stress and increase competence in working with trauma populations.[21]

> *If you have a history of trauma, you should consider utilizing psychotherapy as a self-care practice to discuss and address any unresolved conflicts from your past.*

Chloe's Case: Seeking Support and Guidance

Although Chloe is receiving supervision for her work with a client who has a history of sexual abuse, this is Chloe's first client with a history of trauma. Her supervisor tends to focus on learning about sexual abuse and the logistics of techniques in treating the client. Chloe fears that she will appear "weak" to her supervisor if she brings up difficulties. As a student in training, Chloe wants to receive a positive evaluation from her supervisor and not appear confrontational. Yet it is important for Chloe to express her concerns and experiences and to discuss with her supervisor the nature of working with trauma clients and how this work is impacting her personally. Additionally, Chloe may benefit from participating in group supervision: She can then express her feelings and hear from other graduate student trainees on their experiences in working with their clients. This may help Chloe not only to normalize her reactions and develop an understanding that it is impossible to be "strong enough" to ignore or avoid deeply emotional reactions in her work with this client, but also to focus on properly addressing these reactions. Finally, Chloe may consider entering personal psychotherapy, where she can further explore her feelings regarding her client as well as any personal history that working with this client may be bringing up for Chloe.

Considerations When Working with Trauma Clients and Prevention of Vicarious Trauma and Secondary Traumatic Stress

- Consider your present level of experience and expertise in working with trauma clients.
- Know your past personal vulnerabilities (e.g., history of trauma, personal or family illness, relationship difficulties) and what may be considered warning signs for vicarious trauma and secondary traumatic stress.
- Consider how you may anticipate your past personal vulnerabilities influencing you and your work with your client.
- Consider the effects of current stressors and emotional challenges in your personal and professional life at present.
- Look out for and recognize signs of vicarious trauma and secondary traumatic stress; conduct ongoing self-assessments of warning signs and symptoms.
- Engage in ongoing conversations with supervisors regarding warning signs and symptoms of vicarious trauma and secondary traumatic stress.
- Consider personal psychotherapy
  - as a preventive measure in awareness of potential risk for vicarious trauma and secondary traumatic stress.
  - as a reparative tool when signs of vicarious trauma and secondary traumatic stress are evident.
- Practice ongoing self-care.

Vicarious Trauma and Secondary Traumatic Stress Checklist

The following is an informal checklist of symptoms of vicarious trauma and secondary traumatic stress. Mark off all that currently apply to you.

_____ Experience of recollections or dreams about the client's traumatic event

_____ Preoccupation with a client's traumatic event

_____ Avoidance of reminders of a client's trauma

_____ Loss of interest in pleasurable activities

_____ Hyperarousal (e.g., difficulty sleeping, difficulty concentrating)

_____ Avoidance of clients

_____ Feelings of helplessness or confusion

_____ Increased sense of isolation from support networks

_____ Numbness

_____ Cynicism

Reflection Activity

Reflect on your own personal history. What personal experiences do you bring with you into the treatment room? What clinical presentations would potentially be more difficult for you or require additional self-awareness given your own personal experiences?

How could this potentially influence your work with clients, including clients with traumatic histories?

Now that you have completed the secondary traumatic stress self-assessment, what steps can you take to continue to monitor your risk of secondary traumatic stress?

How might you more actively and effectively address your personal history and vulnerabilities, risk factors, warning signs, and personal reactions to clients in your ongoing supervision?

Are you currently working with a client with a traumatic history? Reflect on this experience.

Have you noticed signs of secondary traumatic stress? What about signs of distress, problems with professional competence, or burnout? What about the impact of issues in your personal life?

If you are not currently experiencing any signs of secondary traumatic stress, what prevention measures can you take to reduce your risk in the future? Reflect on the current level of support you now receive for this work and whether this matches the level of support (e.g., supervision, practicing self-care, personal psychotherapy, support from peers) you believe you need, after having learned about secondary traumatic stress and vicarious traumatization. What other changes can be made?

Part II
Establishing Lifestyles of Self-Care

Practices, Strategies, and Plans

The Great Juggling Act

Learning to Strike a Balance Between Your Professional and Personal Lives

Life Outside the Graduate School Bubble

Josie is a graduate student preparing for the birth of her first child. She is excited about the opportunity to become a mother and has received considerable support from faculty and peers as she works to balance her responsibilities as a student and a soon-to-be parent. However, Josie has felt stressed at times during the pregnancy: She has had to occasionally miss class to attend doctors' appointments and to give up her night-owl hours, when she often completed much of her schoolwork. Josie has also recently been dealing with fatigue at the end of the day, which makes it challenging to attend the evening client appointments she has been assigned. She also is concerned about leaving her clients for three months while she is away on maternity leave. She often stays up at night worrying about how she will be able to balance it all once the baby arrives and how future internship sites may view her as a working mother. She anticipates some challenges in the future in balancing her new family life with her graduate work, but expects that upon return- ing from maternity leave she will be able to continue at her current pace of taking a full course load, working a full schedule at her practicum site, applying for another supervised training position, and working her way toward graduation and licensure. She wants to finish graduate school as soon as possible so that she can begin her career.

The Graduate Student's Many Roles

There is no shortage of responsibilities to juggle as a graduate student. Need we remind you of the classwork, comprehensive exams, group projects, thesis or dissertation, research projects, and teaching assistantships? Then there is the practicum, internship, clinical work with clients, supervision sessions, documentation and other administrative requirements, and involvement in professional organizations. In your personal life, you likely fill numerous roles as friend, sibling, child, spouse, parent, and so forth that bring countless responsibilities. Your identity as a graduate student is thus just one of many that make up who you are.

In addition to the many roles you play in your personal and professional lives, there are also a number of roles and opportunities you may commit to voluntarily. This is particularly true when you are in graduate training, as it can be difficult to say "no" to exciting opportunities that present themselves such as professional writing, presentations, joining research teams, service to university or departmental committees and professional associations, or applying for and working in jobs related to the field.

How can you work to effectively juggle and balance all of these responsibilities while in graduate school? And furthermore, how do you make efforts at balancing without making significant or harmful sacrifices within your personal or professional life? These are challenging questions that you and all graduate students will face throughout your training, and throughout your professional career.

The good news is that balance *is* possible, even in graduate school! Where you choose to set the dial on your own personal balancing act will be unique to you, your life, your roles, your obligations, and your goals and priorities. However, this chapter can help you figure out where to begin establishing or improving balance for yourself.

Balance as a Key Ingredient for Success

Life is never static. Numerous changes will occur within your personal and professional life as a graduate student and later on in your career that will require you to reexamine and alter the ways in which you achieve balance between the personal and professional. It is therefore important to learn about and develop strategies of balance now. You may not be able to take a break from juggling your roles and responsibilities altogether, but effective efforts at achieving this balance will enable you to juggle with greater ease and effectiveness, while also reducing the risk of a misstep and having all that you juggle come crashing to the floor.

You likely have learned throughout your years of schooling that hard work and diligence are the keys to success. Maxims such as "the harder you work, the more successful you will be," and "work hard and sacrifice everything else now for the benefit of a successful career down the road," are common among graduate students. Like many of your peers you may be working hard and striving to do more, seizing every opportunity that presents itself, working to fill up the C.V. or résumé. But are you able to recognize when the load becomes too heavy, when your work is no longer providing you with the degree of success and satisfaction you hoped for? Working hard to the exclusion or neglect of other important aspects of your life can actually paradoxically result in less success in graduate school and, in turn, less success in your career!

Balance plays a key role in the prevention of burnout.[1] Therefore, learning to balance your personal and professional lives in ways that both attend to your professional goals and demands, while also tending to your personal relationships and interests, can contribute to your success and well-being. Remember that as a psychologist in training you are in many ways your own tool in the services you provide to others. Balance and efforts to take care of yourself are akin to the care and maintenance of instruments used by other professionals in their work.[2] As a goal of graduate school moves beyond becoming a successful student to developing a successful professional identity, consider the ways in which balance between your personal and professional lives, and even within each, will be part of your professional identify. "Responsibly taking care of ourselves, as well as our patients, may be the most important thing we do, not just for ourselves, but ultimately for our clients, and for our own families."[3]

The Personal-Professional Interaction

It is important to understand how your professional and personal lives interact with each other. As we have discussed, the personal and professional aspects of your life are not two separate domains that exist in isolation. As humans, we live in neither professional nor personal vacuums; problems in our professional and personal realms can flow into and influence each other.[4] There is no barrier that separates the two, and each regularly impacts the other.

For example, feeling distressed over the recent death of a loved one may impact your ability to effectively work with clients. Likewise, stress in the professional domain, such as a receiving a poor evaluation from a supervisor or learning that a client has committed suicide, can easily impact your personal life and relationships;[5] you might come home from school and argue with your partner or loved one or be emotionally withdrawn and unable to meet the emotional needs of those you care about.[6] Figure 5.1 shows how the various aspects of your personal and professional life not only individually influence you, but also continuously interact, creating a constantly rotating cycle of personal and professional demands and roles impacting your life—a great juggling act indeed!

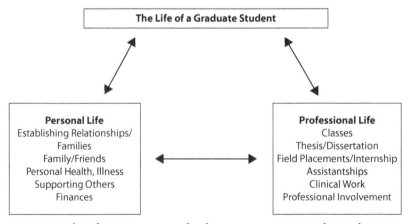

FIGURE 5.1 This chart represents the dynamic interaction of a graduate student's personal and professional roles and responsibilities.

But how do you work to achieve balance between your personal and professional lives? It would be impossible to create imperme-able dividers, blocking any interaction between them. Instead, improved management of this great juggling act starts with the following tips:

- Seek appropriate support during times of heightened stress or difficulty. For example, talk with fellow students or to peer support groups about school or clinical issues to help reduce bringing home some of that stress to family and partners.
- Create schedules that go beyond graduate school commitments. While not everything in your life can be scheduled, and things may come up last minute, having a schedule for appointments and activities in your personal life can help to ensure that you find the time to attend to them. This can include everything from an upcoming oil change for your car to a weekly date night.
- Unwind. You may often walk in the door still carrying the load of the day's responsibilities and, if working clinically, clients' issues, but taking just 5 minutes to unwind can help remove some of the day's stress and help you transition from your professional to personal responsibilities. This 5 minutes means truly disconnecting—no checking e-mail, no answering phone calls, and so forth. Use the time to reflect on the day, listen to music, watch television, meditate— whatever may work for you. If it is not possible to find 5 minutes of unwinding time after you walk in the door, be creative to find other available times, such as your car ride home from school or work.

The ongoing juggling act and interaction between the personal and professional domains can also be a good thing. For example, your professional work can contribute to feelings of personal growth, which in turn positively influence your personal relationships and overall life satisfaction.[7] You may also experience positive feelings and personal satisfaction because your work has positively impacted others' lives and provided solutions to human problems.[8] Keep an eye out, therefore, for the positive outcomes of the natural interaction between your personal and professional domains while you work to minimize potential negative outcomes.

Voice of Experience: One Psychologist's Perspective

Once, when working with two actively suicidal clients simultaneously, I found myself becoming increasingly frustrated with
how demanding my family was and with how little they seemed
to appreciate how hard I worked. I would arrive home in the
evening after a difficult day and become very frustrated with
all their demands. After a short time I was informed that *they*
hadn't changed at all: *I* was the one acting differently. It didn't
take much introspection for me to realize that I was stressed,
overwhelmed, and more than a bit scared working with these
clients. Just realizing this felt like a significant relief and was
the first step in taking positive actions to get more support and
assistance in working with these challenging clients.

Work-Family Conflict

If you are attempting to balance graduate school professional life
with personal roles in your family, welcome to the work-family conflict. As you may have already experienced, this is a reciprocal relationship in which the demands of each domain are often in conflict.[9]
Many psychologists today are facing this struggle. Too little time and
energy left after work to devote to family was recently reported as the
most common stressor among professional psychologists.[10] Marriage
and relationship problems were two of the top five reported personal
problems endorsed by surveyed marriage and family therapists.[11]

Examples of work-family conflict may include on-call coverage
requirements at your training site impacting planning for family activities; time spent on thesis, dissertation, or report writing
(often reserved for evenings and weekends) spilling over into family
time; and having to schedule clients during evening hours, which
can be particularly challenging for those with children. The seemingly never-ending readings, term papers, clinical hours, meetings,
and other school-related activities can also regularly take over family time. Family members or significant others who have difficulty
understanding the amount of work you must devote to your academic and clinical obligations outside of the regular 9-to-5 workday
may add additional strain.

Also consider any additional roles you have taken on beyond those required for graduate school and training—these can include conducting research, writing articles, giving presentations, attending conferences, assuming leadership positions in professional organizations or on boards, and many more. While helpful in enhancing your professional development, they also divert time and attention from other areas of your life.

Graduate school does not have set work hours. Often this results in the feeling that there is always more to do—and more you can do in your ongoing effort to earn high grades, develop important clinical skills and knowledge, and build your professional identity. Negotiating just where work ends and family or personal time begins can be an especially vexing challenge. Take some time to review and evaluate your professional development obligations. Consider the following questions:

- Are you able to manage your obligations along with your other professional and personal responsibilities?
- If you have experienced difficulties balancing them with other responsibilities, how have you felt about this?
- What changes can be made to assist you with your responsibilities? For example, if on a committee, can you share the workload with another committee member? Can the committee consider taking on another member to assist in the workload? Are you able to do your work individually and at times that work for you? Or do you work as a group, meeting at times that may interfere with other personal or professional demands?
- Also, consider whether you have taken on too much. Do all of your professional development responsibilities fit with your goals? If not, consider the value of certain responsibilities in exchange for your current attempts at balancing your personal and professional lives.

Guidelines for Establishing and Maintaining Balance in Graduate School

It can be difficult at first to identify where to begin or what roles or responsibilities you can try to change when it comes to achieving balance. You may at times feel that neglecting or walking away from roles and responsibilities is the only way to achieve balance—but this really is not balance at all. Instead, remember that just like the other aspects of psychological wellness we have discussed, balancing the personal and professional aspects of your life is an ongoing, lifelong process that will require alterations throughout the different stages of your life and career.

"It's an ongoing process to learn, find, practice, maintain, and regain our balance."[12] Furthermore, balance is not achieved overnight, nor is it realistic to expect yourself to successfully and evenly balance all the personal and professional areas of your life at all times. Rather, viewing your efforts at balance as a dynamic and everchanging, ever-improving process will enable you to begin making progress toward achieving a more balanced lifestyle.

The following is a list of guidelines and tips on attaining and improving balance in your personal and professional life.

- Figure out what you are juggling.
  - Identify the roles, responsibilities, and tasks in your personal and professional lives.
  - Refer back to Chapter 1, "Exploring Your Sources of Distress," for a helpful list of your self-identified current roles and obligations.
- Identify priorities and non-priorities.
  - Consider the priorities in your personal life—eating dinner with your family, making sure to pick up your children from day care on time each day, attending your weekly yoga class, and so forth.
  - Consider the priorities in your professional life. While academic responsibilities are priorities you must fulfill, make a full examination of your volunteer commitments, meetings, times spend on academic work, and so forth to establish your true priorities.
  - Return to your list of roles and responsibilities. Having now identified your priorities, what remains on the list? What can be changed about the remaining roles and responsibilities? For example, can they be removed, can you do them less frequently, can you find alternative times to complete these tasks, can you ask for help?
- Balance the professional realm.

- Develop or maintain a degree of control over your work by establishing limits and boundaries on professional demands and tasks and developing realistic expectations.[13]
- Schedule time for breaks—daily breaks, lunch breaks, relaxation/recreation, periodic vacations.[14]
- Disconnect—schedule allotted time to check e-mail, listen to voicemail messages, or complete assignments during weekends, extended holidays, and vacations to avoid working all day, every day.[15]
- Talk to your supervisor about maintaining your caseload at a manageable level.[16]
- Allot specific times for completing work, giving your best effort and attention during that time, and stop when time is up.
- Use your time wisely—consider your goals when allotting time to complete a task. Is your goal of earning an A on the exam important enough to get by on 5 hours of sleep, or can you accept an A– to get 8 hours of sleep?
- Balance the personal realm.
  - Do not wait for free or personal time to come around. Carve out reserved time on a regular basis to spend with family members and friends (e.g., Thursday night dinner with friends, date nights every other Saturday).
  - Set appropriate boundaries in your personal relationships regarding your roles and responsibilities. This means committing to your responsibilities without also committing to the responsibilities of others. This may require saying "no" at times when asked to take on more. Consider saying something such as "While I would love to help and appreciate you asking, I am already fully committed with my own responsibilities and would not be able to offer the assistance you are looking for."
  - Set limits on personal time to avoid using it as an excuse to ignore or delay addressing professional responsibilities.
  - Be creative! Look for appropriate ways to combine aspects of your personal and professional life simultaneously (e.g., study sessions with peers, creating social events with cohort, working out with partner).

Avoid a one-size-fits-all approach to balance; what works for another individual may not necessarily work for you. None of us enjoys more than 24 hours in a day and we all have only 100% of ourselves to divide up. However, how you choose to divide your time and for what purposes is what makes balance unique to each and every individual.

Josie and the Work-Family Conflict

Josie's pregnancy and future role as a mother is one example of the work-family conflict. Josie's academic and clinical obligations have made it challenging for her to attend to all that she would like to do in preparation for the birth of her child, and she is concerned about how she will find the time once the baby is born to complete her academic responsibilities while also being there for her family. It is important that Josie take time to examine her current and future responsibilities and consider what changes can be made to better balance the personal and professional and to prioritize the roles and obligations within her busy life. Josie can talk with her supervisor about these concerns and ask whether it is possible to schedule earlier client appointments. Josie can also talk to peers and faculty who may be able to relate to Josie's experience and offer her realistic expectations for meeting all of her obligations and roles. Josie may benefit from mapping out the hours each day she will need complete schoolwork, ensuring that the schedule allows for personal time. Josie may also evaluate her current course load and client load and may choose to reduce these on a temporary or permanent basis when she returns from maternity leave. Josie may be able to develop a time line with faculty to provide her with extended time to complete her program requirements. Regarding future training positions, Josie may be interested in pursuing sites that offer part-time training opportunities.

Reflection Activity

Reflect on your current personal and professional roles. To what degree do you work to achieve balance in these realms?

If there is imbalance, where does the imbalance lie?

What changes can you make to begin making steps toward balancing or to continue to improve your efforts at balancing the personal and professional?

Reflect on any obstacles you may anticipate regarding putting these plans to balance into action.

What are some of the benefits you may potentially experience from making such changes in your personal and professional lives?

Weekly Balance Action Plan

The following table provides an example of Josie's weekly schedule, created for after she gives birth and returns from maternity leave. It reflects her efforts at balancing schoolwork with family time. After reviewing her schedule, take time to consider your weekly schedule. To what extent does it include attempts at balancing both your professional and personal life? Use the blank calendar provided to sketch a weekly schedule that you can begin to follow. Include your personal and professional obligations while also making active efforts and adjustments to your current schedule to achieve a more well balanced lifestyle, one that reflects many of the self-care practices for achieving balance reviewed in this chapter.

Josie's Weekly Planner

Mon	Tues	Wed	Thurs	Fri	Sat	Sun
5–8 a.m.: Wake up, feed baby, get ready	5–7:30 a.m.: Wake up, feed baby, get ready	5–7:30 a.m.: Wake up, feed baby, get ready	5–7:30 a.m.: Wake up, feed baby, get ready	5–7:30 a.m.: Wake up, feed baby, get ready	8 a.m.–12 p.m.: Homework (husband takes care of baby in a.m.)	5–7:30 a.m.: Wake up, feed baby
9–11 a.m.: Class	8 a.m.–12 p.m.: Class	8–9 a.m.: Spin class	8 a.m.–1 p.m.: Practicum	8–9 a.m.: Weekly dissertation meeting		Sun a.m.: Call family, run errands, do chores
12–1 p.m.: Call to check on Aunt Rose	12–1 p.m.:	10–4 p.m.: Practicum	1–4:30 p.m.: Homework	9–4 p.m.: Work on dissertation		
LUNCH	LUNCH check e-mails	LUNCH (11:30 a.m.–12 p.m.)	LUNCH (1–1:30 p.m.)	LUNCH (11:30 a.m.–12 p.m.)	12–5pm: Family time	Sun p.m.: Dinner with family Prep for the upcoming week
1–4 p.m.: Supervision Practicum	1–4 p.m.: Class					
4:30–8:30 p.m.: Family time Dinner	4:30–8:30 p.m.: Family time Dinner	4:30–8:30 p.m.: Family time, Dinner	4:30–8:30 p.m.: Family time, Dinner	4:30–11 p.m.: Family time	5 p.m.: Dinner with friends or date night with husband	
8:30–11 p.m.: Check e-mails Homework	8:30–11 p.m.: Check e-mails Homework	8:30–11pm: Check e-mails Homework	8:30–11 p.m.: Check e-mails Homework			

My Weekly Balance Action Plan

Mon	Tues	Wed	Thurs	Fri	Sat	Sun

Get a Great Mentor Now!

Who Needs a Mentor Anyway?

Erika has just completed her first year of graduate school. While she has worked with academic advisors throughout her academic life, she has not engaged in a mentoring relationship. Erika finds herself with many questions and uncertainties regarding her training and professional future, such as figuring out where to apply for her next practicum placement, becoming more professionally involved in the field, navigating the research process that she has just begun, and deciding on a specific career path within the mental health field. She is anxious about being a new clinician with her first caseload embarking on her first psychotherapy sessions. Erika thought that during her time in graduate school a professor would possibly seek her out to "take her under his or her wing" and begin a mentoring relationship, but she is now realizing that she needs to take the initiative to obtain a mentor. However, Erika does not know where to begin to find a mentor, what makes for a good mentor, or what she can expect from the mentoring relationship that will add to or be different from her relationships with her academic advisor, her supervisors, or personal psychotherapist.

Mentoring 101

As you work to develop your professional identity during graduate school, you will increasingly engage in countless academic and professional activities that will eventually result in your transformation from student to seasoned psychologist. Yet it may also feel as though you are maneuvering through this developmental process in the dark. Mentoring relationships during graduate school can offer you the opportunity to receive guidance and support that can be personally and professionally enriching and that can greatly enhance your graduate school experience. Read on for an extensive list of benefits that having a good mentor can provide.

From academic advisors to professors, supervisors, and principal investigators, you likely have had and will continue to have many professional relationships over the course of your graduate training. With all of these relationships available to you, what makes mentoring different, and why is it so important? Unlike supervisors or advisors whose goals are to promote your development within the parameters of your role within that relationship (e.g., as a supervisee, as a student), "a mentor proactively seeks to enhance the development and education of a protégé."[1]

> *Unlike supervisors or advisors whose goals are to promote your development within the parameters of your role within that relationship, "a mentor proactively seeks to enhance the development and education of a protégé."*

Mentoring is a personal relationship between a more experienced faculty member or professional and a less experienced graduate student or junior professional, in which mentors serve as a "guide, role model, teacher, and sponsor."[2] Career and psychosocial development are the two main functions mentoring relationships can serve for you as a mentee.[3] Mentors can provide you with knowledge, expertise, and experience while serving as role models, offering opportunities to engage in career enhancing professional activities, and providing advice and support.[4]

The mentoring relationship is also reciprocal: Mentors will not only share expertise, opportunities, and support with you, but also have an opportunity to learn from you, adding to the uniqueness of the mentoring dynamic.[5] The ongoing growth of the mentoring relationship and the numerous and multifaceted functions it serves further highlight the valuable nature of mentoring beginning in graduate school and throughout your professional career.

Did You Know...

- Sixty-six percent of American Psychological Association member-psychologists who had graduated with a PhD or PsyD in the mid-1990s had a faculty mentor while in graduate school.[6]
- Ninety-one percent of mentees reported that their mentoring relationship was either extremely or moderately positive.[7]
- Mentees in counseling psychology programs reported the highest levels of socio-emotional support from their mentoring relationships among graduate students in counseling, clinical, and experimental graduate programs.[8]
- Mentees in clinical and experimental graduate programs endorsed the benefit of instrumental and research-related support from their mentoring.[9]

Benefits of Mentorship

The benefits of mentoring can be invaluable to your overall success not only as a graduate student, but continuing on into your professional role as a psychologist. The variety and depth of these benefits exemplify how mentoring relationships contribute beyond other academic or professional relationships within which you may receive guidance or supervision.

Professional Development and Training Benefits

- Mentors and mentees have the opportunity to share experiences, perspectives, and frustrations experienced in training and professional work.[10]
- Mentors can provide assistance in professional training and career development (e.g., goal setting, networking opportunities, conference invitations).

- Mentees can receive support with both professional and identity development.[11]
- For mentees who identify as members of racial, ethnic, sexual, or other minority groups, mentors adequately trained in relevant diversity experiences may provide the following:
  - Guidance and support
  - Assistance in navigating and tending to the psychosocial development of the mentee's professional career
  - Help with navigating potential challenges or issues (e.g., discrimination, stigma)[12]
- Mentoring relationships may also contribute to skill development enhancement, an overall greater satisfaction with your graduate training program, and assistance and support in identifying and realizing your professional goals.[13]

Self-Care and Psychological Wellness Benefits

- Mentors can serve as models for appropriately balancing professional demands and personal life, preventing problems of professional competence, and practicing self-care strategies.[14]
- Mentors and mentees have the opportunity to exchange perspectives on managing graduate school demands, internship, and post-doc experiences.

Benefits Beyond Graduate School

- Assistance with navigating postgraduate school hurdles:
  - Licensure or certification processes
  - Networking opportunities/career planning/employment acquisition
  - Establishment of a practice
  - Financial planning resources for student loans or building a practice
- Psychologists who identified as being a mentee at one time in their professional development reported more positive performance evaluations, higher salaries, and faster career progress than those who had not been mentored.[15]

Voice of Experience: One Psychologist's Perspective

I have had a number of great mentors throughout my career. While each one provided me with something different, they had several features in common. Each person was someone I respected, someone who was a great role model professionally as well as with regard to balance within and between professional and personal lives, and someone who really took an interest in me—demonstrating genuine caring about my professional development and providing me with opportunities for professional involvement and advancement. These relationships enriched my experience professionally and personally, and were instrumental in my professional growth and development. They each showed me "the ropes," introduced me to their colleagues, and included me in their professional networks, and they helped me to understand what it truly means to be a professional psychologist. Each of them influenced me as a psychologist and as a person. I carry their influence with me today, both in how I live and in how I mentor others.

Goals in the Mentoring Relationship

Before beginning to seek out a mentor, assess your needs and goals for the mentoring relationship. While the areas of support you may receive from a mentor may shift over time to adjust to the changes and growth of your professional career, you will probably seek a mentor who can address your areas of greatest need or guidance. For example, if you are in a heavily research-based graduate program with a professional goal of obtaining a faculty position at a university, you may not benefit much from working with a mentor who currently works in full-time private practice, compared to a full-time faculty member. Instead, you may benefit more from a mentor in the research community who holds a faculty position. Unlike conversations with your advisor or principal investigator, which may generally focus on your current research and graduate student goals, conversations with a mentor may include dealing with the struggles and pressures of getting published and

Conversations with a mentor may include dealing with the struggles and pressures of getting published and eventually tenured, navigating the nature of academic environments and faculty relationships, and managing the transition from graduate student to faculty member.

eventually tenured, navigating the nature of academic environments and faculty relationships, and managing the transition from graduate student to faculty member.

Obtaining a Mentor

After reviewing all the potential benefits of mentoring relationships, it is easy to see why so many students would like to have mentors during their graduate school years and beyond. But how do you get a good mentor? Do you find your mentor, or can you wait to see whether he or she will find you? What follows are some important steps to take that can help make this process easier.

Identifying Mentor Candidates

Mentoring relationships are typically developed in one of two ways—formally or informally. Formal mentoring is typically offered through organizations, programs, or associations and utilizes a match process to pair you with a mentor.[16] (See the next section for more information on formal mentoring programs.) Informal mentoring develops more organically, either on your initiative or your mentor's. Often informal mentoring results from an already established relationship with a more senior person in the field.[17]

Take some time now to consider any faculty or other senior professionals with whom you share interests or find it easy to talk to, or who present positive characteristics that suggest the individual may make a strong mentor (e.g., genuine interest in graduate student development, good communication skills, collegial nature in relationships with graduate students, positive self-care practices). Then actively seek out and speak to these individuals about their interest in participating in an informal mentoring process. For example, if you know of a faculty member who is very involved in governance activities and leadership roles within the profession and this is something that interests you, this would be a good professional to meet with. If a faculty member regularly publishes articles and gives conference presentations with students and this coincides with your goals, he or she might be a good mentor for you.

How can you approach establishing a mentoring relationship? Seeking out a mentor can feel like an intimidating experience, especially as you likely will view your mentor and the mentor's work in high esteem. Here are a few suggestions on how to find a mentor and how to navigate the initial phase of establishing a mentoring relationship:

- Look for potential mentors both within and outside of your graduate program. Faculty members, advisors, or supervisors can serve as great mentors. So too can early career or seasoned psychologists working outside of your graduate program.
- Take advantage of conferences, meetings, and other professional forums to initiate conversation with those in the field. Not sure what to talk about? Ask them about their work, or share your experience as a graduate student. Remember that these psychologists were once graduate students too, and are often open to sharing their professional development journey with students. This may serve as an opportunity to meet a potential mentor.
- Join a professional committee or a membership group that reflects an area of the field you are interested in or wish to pursue in your career. Being in the presence of psychologists who share similar interests to you is a great place to begin establishing professional relationships and possibly a mentoring relationship.
- Ask around. Inquire from seasoned peers in your graduate program or practicum site about their mentoring experiences. They may be able to recommend psychologists in your department or within the professional community whose interests match yours or who are interested in serving as a mentor.

Formal Mentorship Opportunities

Student memberships of several APA divisions, including those listed below, as well as some state psychological associations and other professional organizations, offer member benefits including mentoring programs or opportunities for students to become active members in these groups which offer chances to get to know and work alongside seasoned professionals. Even if formal mentoring opportunities are not offered, you can use your membership in these organizations to seek out informal mentoring opportunities, such as volunteering at a conference or event and meeting with and working with leaders of the profession.

- APA's Division 15 (Educational Psychology) (www.apadiv15.org)
- APA's Division 17 (Counseling Psychology) (www.div17.org)
- APA's Division 29, Psychotherapy (www. divisionofpsychotherapy.org)
- APA's Division 38 (Health Psychology)—specifically for those interested in women's health (www.health-psych.org)
- APA's Division 39 (Psychoanalysis) (www.apadivisions.org/ division-39)
- APA's Division 40, Clinical Neuropsychology (www.div40.org)
- APA's Division 42, Psychologists in Independent Practice (www.division42.org).
- APA's Division 43, Family Psychology (www.division43apa.org)
- APA's Division 52, International Psychology (www.div52.org)
- APA's Disability Issues Office (http://www.apa.org/pi/ disability/resources/mentoring/about.aspx)
- The American Psychological Association of Graduate Students (APAGS) (www.apa.org/apags)

Within APAGS, several committees and groups also offer mentoring opportunities:
- APAGS Committee on LGBT Concerns (APAGS-CLGBTC) (http://www.apa.org/apags/governance/subcommittees/clgbtc-mentoring-program.aspx)
- APAGS Committee on Ethnic Minority Affairs (APAGS-CEMA) (http://www.apa.org/apags/governance/ subcommittees/cema-strategic-plan.aspx)

One Student's Mentoring Experience

I (LC) have been fortunate to have the opportunity to work with and learn from two wonderful mentors during graduate school. Because these mentors have a variety of experiences and expertise, I am able to explore and address the breadth of my own professional interests. My primary mentor, who had been one of my teachers during the first year of graduate school, mentors me not only in my clinical, research, and academic areas of interest, but also in the development of my professional identity and involvement in the field. We have worked collaboratively on professional writing and conference presentations, and he has assisted me in obtaining leadership positions within the profession. My second mentor, an early career psychologist whom I met through my involvement in my state psychological association, has been a source of support and guidance as I journey through this maze of graduate school and preparation for professional life after graduate school. She also serves as a role model in practicing work-life balance in the postgraduate phase. As a neophyte attempting to understand and carve a place for myself in the profession, these mentors continue to play an invaluable role in assisting me to navigate my development into this profession and achieve my goals.

What Makes for an Effective Mentor?

Commonly, mentees will seek out mentors with shared demographic characteristics (e.g., gender, race, religion, or sexual orientation) and who have values, attitudes, and experiences that are shared or desired by the mentee.[18] Effective mentors exhibit qualities such as intelligence, appropriate amounts of humor, flexibility, empathy, and patience[19]—something to keep in mind when you are considering potential mentors.

Effective mentors exhibit qualities such as intelligence, appropriate amounts of humor, flexibility, empathy, and patience—something to keep in mind when you are considering potential mentors.

The ability to set boundaries is also important in mentoring relationships, and it is an essential quality of an effective mentor. While mentoring relationships may be close, with open sharing of personal information and significant amounts of time together, effective mentors never overstep the mentoring role and do not take advantage of the trust their mentees put in them. Successful and ethical mentoring relationships tend to share two key characteristics: Participants establish clear expectations from the beginning regarding what each participant will get out of the relationship, and they ensure that clear and consistent boundaries are established and maintained.[20]

Being a Successful Mentee

Setting Clear Goals

While the mentoring relationship can play a critical role in both your psychological wellness and the development of your professional identity, its success is dependent on the efforts of both the mentor and the mentee. "Shared assumptions and expectations" from both mentor and mentee are the cornerstone of successful graduate school mentoring relationships.[21] Be open with mentors from the beginning about your expectations and goals for the mentoring relationship and how the mentor can best help you achieve your goals. Communicate openly and offer feedback throughout the course of the relationship. This will help to minimize the chance of either party being disappointed.

Being Respectful and Professional

Respect for your mentor and the mentoring relationship is important.[22] This includes respect for your mentor's limited time as well as for your mentor as a whole. Arrive on time for meetings or appointments, and maintain professional etiquette in communication (e.g., e-mails) even when this relationship may seem friendlier or more personal than your other professional relationships.[23] Convey appreciation to your mentor for opportunities provided that are outside of what is normally expected. Remember, the mentoring relationship is not a one-way street.

Maintaining Appropriate Boundaries

While you will be looking to your mentor for guidance, maintain a balance of support and individuality with him or her.[24] The mentoring relationship should not become one of psychotherapy or clinical supervision. Instead, a mentor should serve as a source of support and guidance, a sounding board, a source of professional development opportunities, and a professional role model. Use your mentor as a guide to help you achieve your goals; do not rely on him or her for hand-holding every step of the way. Appropriately use the resources and contacts your mentor may provide, be appropriately appreciative, and be careful not to drain your mentor of his or her time or resources. This demonstrates your level of professionalism and respect for your mentor.

Being Actively Involved in the Mentoring Experience

Finally, maintain an engaged and proactive role in the relationship with your mentor. Mentor involvement levels will vary. While it is important that you and your mentor establish reasonable expectations for the degree of involvement and engagement between the two of you, it is up to you to set up meetings with your mentor, to reach out when you have questions, and so forth. Do not wait for your mentor to contact you. Mentors are often more than willing to devote their time and attention to the professional growth of those beginning in the field. However, given the countless demands and activities these psychologists juggle, it is important for mentees to take the initiative in nurturing this unique and highly beneficial relationship.

Tips on Mentoring

- Reflect on and establish your professional interests and goals when choosing a mentor.
- Consider current positive professional relationships you have with faculty, supervisors, or advisors with whom you may share similar interests or goals, and set up a meeting if you are interested in a mentoring relationship with any of these professionals.
- Talk with classmates. Ask them whether they have mentors and who they recommend among faculty as mentors.
- It is okay to think outside the box when it comes to mentoring, and you can have more than one mentor to meet your varied needs and goals. Establishing relationships with practicing psychologists, early career psychologists, or other

professionals outside of your training program can also provide a wealth of knowledge and expertise and serve as a source of support apart from your graduate program.

- Keep in mind the characteristics of effective mentors. Entering a mentoring relationship is a commitment; take time to reflect on questions such as the following:
  - To what degree do this professional and I share similar interests?
  - Does this professional appear to be able to provide his or her knowledge, past experience, or resources in assisting me to reach my professional goals?
  - Does this mentor currently have the time and availability to take on a mentee?
- Be open discussing and establishing clear goals and expectations with your mentor regarding the mentoring relationship.
- Be proactive! Take initiative in reaching out to your mentor and maintaining an ongoing relationship.
- Always demonstrate respect and professionalism toward your mentor.

Erika's Quest for a Mentor

It is important for Erika to take some time to consider who may best be able to meet her mentoring needs. Because she wants to obtain guidance in the clinical aspects of her professional career and get involved in professional organizations, she may benefit from contacting her local psychology professional organizations and graduate student organizations to ask about being formally matched with a seasoned psychologist. Erika could also schedule a meeting with her academic advisor or other close faculty members to discuss her goals and areas of interest, and to ask if he or she can provide any suggestions for who may be a strong match in a mentoring relationship. Finally, Erika could attend networking events, conferences, and other events hosted by professional organizations to increase her involvement in the field and to begin establishing connections with seasoned professionals who may be interested in offering their time and expertise to Erika and establishing a mentoring relationship.

Creating a Mentor Action Plan

Complete the action plan below to assist you in taking steps toward obtaining a mentor.

1. My current clinical and research interests:

2. My academic and professional goals:

3. Three to five areas of my graduate training or professional identity that I am challenged by, interested in learning more about, or feel that I would benefit from speaking to a mentor about:

4. List of professionals and organizations I can contact to inquire regarding seeking a mentoring relationship:

5. Qualities, attributes, and expertise I am looking for in a mentor:

6. Opportunities I would like to have that a mentor might help me to access:

Reflection Activity

Returning to the notion of self-care, consider how mentoring can now relate to your efforts to improve your overall psychological wellness by answering the following questions:

1. Engaging in mentoring relationships is considered a form of self-care. What specific ways do you believe you can benefit from mentoring as a self-care strategy and improve your overall psychological wellness?

2. Actively participating in a mentoring relationship as a mentee can include attending meetings with your mentor, attending professional events, and so forth. Considering the additional time commitment required by a mentoring relationship, reflect on any challenges you may anticipate regarding your psychological wellness (e.g., issues with balancing personal and professional time). What can you do to address these challenges?

The Graduate School Marathon

Goal Setting, Time Management, and Creating Realistic Expectations for Success

Where's the Road Map? Charting the Course for Graduate School and Beyond

After earning two master's degrees, working several years in a research lab, and balancing all this with a part-time job, Ben felt both ready and eager to begin his doctoral program. Upon reviewing his course syllabi and planning out his programmatic obligations, Ben feels overwhelmed with the tasks and responsibilities he has ahead of him and wonders whether he will be able to accomplish it all. He feels that every time he starts to attend to a project or assignment, he becomes distracted with the accruing list of other tasks he has to take care of within his academic program—in addition to obligations at his job, with his family, and other personal tasks. Additionally, Ben feels that he has "tunnel vision" and devotes all of his time and energy to keeping up with the day-to-day tasks of his program, making it difficult to think about and make progress toward his long-term career goals. Ben is also unclear about how to plan out the next five years of his doctoral program, including beginning an action plan for his dissertation, worrying that he is already behind his classmates. Recently, Ben has experienced several migraines, he has difficulty sleeping some nights, and he finds himself "running on empty" by the end of each day. Focused on staying on top of his schoolwork, he wonders whether he will ever be able to look past the sea of unending work and have the opportunity to think about or the energy to attend to larger professional goals and aspirations.

Navigating a Sea of Demands

It is a Sunday morning and you are just about to sit down to work on your research paper that is due the next day. Although you had hoped to start earlier, you feel confident because you have allotted all day to devote to finishing this project. After first reading through your e-mails and checking the latest updates on your favorite social networking sites, you settle into your work, only to get a phone call from a classmate asking to brainstorm some ideas about the project with you. She then reminds you of a homework assignment for another class you had forgotten about that is also due tomorrow and you immediately begin working on that. Once that is finished you start on your research paper again, when your significant other walks in the door and asks why you are spending another Sunday doing work instead of spending time together.

Before you know it, it is 4 p.m. and you realize you have almost no food in the house and need to go to the grocery store for the week ahead. After returning home from the store, you eat dinner; it is now 7 p.m. and you are finally returning to work on this paper. Having originally planned to work all day, you had hoped to get this paper done by 5 p.m. and make it to your favorite class at the gym. But, realizing that you are far from finished with the paper, you know the class at the gym will have to wait for another day. You look at the clock, wonder where the time has gone, and realize that it is going to be another late night of work.

Sound familiar? You and nearly every graduate student have likely experienced some version of this story. As you are faced with countless demands and tasks, a list that seems to continue to grow with each day, you are consistently pulled in numerous directions and are forced to make decisions regarding which to attend to first—a point that we continue to return to throughout this book. Whether it is reading for class, writing papers, completing research projects, doing training activities, applying for internship, working on professional development opportunities, or attending to personal activities and obligations—you are confronted by and challenged with a seemingly unending number of responsibilities. Like Ben, it can become difficult at times to navigate these demands effectively and to also look beyond them to attend to the larger or more long term tasks you have ahead of you, as well as to other goals you hope to achieve for yourself.

Setting and Maintaining Goals in the Midst of Graduate School

When you feel you are drowning in the sea of demands presented to you as a graduate student, how do you maintain your focus on the path ahead? Do you feel the need to work on multiple tasks simultaneously, to view each and every task with the same degree of importance and priority, or do you feel intimidated or unclear of where to even begin, resulting in a delay in attending to these tasks? Establishing goals and consistently working to make progress toward these goals are effective means of assisting you in navigating your responsibilities and demands. With so many demands and opportunities as a graduate student, goal setting can assist you in the following:

- Establishing priorities
- Making progress toward both your required and desired objectives
- Providing a sense of purpose and direction and mold your professional identity[1]

While motivation to attain your goals is one necessary component of goal setting,[2] goals require much more than simply the motivation to attain them. Regardless of the type of goal you are creating for yourself (short-term versus long-term; professional versus personal), there are four key factors that are important to consider

Establishing goals and consistently working to make progress toward these goals are effective means of assisting you in navigating your responsibilities and demands.

for successful goal setting.[3] Listed here are the four key factors, with associated examples from Ben's goal of completing his dissertation prior to going on internship.

Four Key Factors for Successful Goal Setting

1. Specific: It involves planning the detailed steps involved in reaching the goal.
   - Example: Ben can break down his goal of completing his dissertation into smaller, specific goals of finding a chair, collecting articles, writing a literature review, and so forth.
2. Realistic: The goal is practical.
   - Example: Ben should determine a realistic amount of time to work on his dissertation each week when considering *all* his obligations, tasks, and self-care. While ideal to work 5 hours per day, that is not realistic given his schedule.
3. Measurable: Goals can be tracked and progress can be marked along the way as you work toward the final goal.
   - Example: Ben can set a measurable goal of sending an updated dissertation draft to his dissertation chair every two months. This will both track Ben's progress and help him work toward his main goal of completing his dissertation.
4. Attainable: The goal is achievable.
   - Example: While Ben may be interested in studying a very unique and specific population for his dissertation, it may be nearly impossible to attain a reasonable sample. Considering his goal of completing his dissertation before going on internship, he should work with his advisor to choose a topic that is practical and can be accomplished.

But What Are My Goals? Making a Values Statement

Completing required research projects, accruing necessary clinical hours, securing practicum sites and/or internship, graduating from the program, and beginning your career are likely among the goals you have set for yourself during the course of your graduate career. Yet, you may also be considering countless other academic, professional, and personal goals, both short and long term, unique to your interests, career goals, personal life, and more. It can be challenging to develop your goals or know which are right for you. Setting big picture goals, such as obtaining your degree, can be broken down into smaller goals to be worked on and achieved over the long term.

Just as many corporations and institutions create mission statements to express their purpose, goals, and ideals, creating a personal values statement can be an important preliminary step in setting goals for yourself. A values statement can include your strengths and talents, your character, and your mission and personal attitudes.[4] Including goals that align with these underlying values can provide a sense of direction and motivation to work toward goals that are both enriching and rewarding for you.[5] Ben's values statement is provided here as an example.

Ben's Values Statement

- I will approach each day as an opportunity to continue to grow and learn as a student and professional.
- I will take each day as it comes and not get overwhelmed by what lies ahead, doing my best to be prepared yet also understanding that not everything is within my control.
- When faced with challenges and obstacles, I will remain focused on my passion of being a helper and healer for others to help guide me through.
- I will not lose sight of my value for family, friends, and self.
- I will do my best to maintain balance in my life and strive to stay connected to all that is important to me, remembering that no singular task or role is my sole identity.

Applying Goal Setting to Your Life

How can you specifically use goal setting in your daily life as a graduate student? Setting goals to help achieve specific objectives can be used in all areas of your life—academic, professional, and personal. Goals can even be used to help with the early incorporation of self-care regimens into hectic schedules.

Goals can be either short term (e.g., daily, weekly, monthly) or long term (e.g., semester long, one year, three years, during graduate school, during your career). In addition to daily, weekly, and monthly goals, short-term goals can also be used as intermediate steps toward achieving long-term goals by breaking down larger goals into more manageable and intermediate steps. For example, Ben's goal of successfully defending his dissertation prior to beginning internship can include a number of short-term goals, such as selecting a topic, finding a chairperson, conducting the literature review, designing the study, finding a sample, collecting data, analyzing the data, and writing and editing dissertation drafts.

Long-term goals, such as semester-long goals, yearly goals, goals to accomplish while in graduate school, or even longer career goals, can play a significant role in helping you to look beyond the daily or immediate tasks at hand. Keep in mind that there may be numerous different ways of achieving these long-term goals. One graduate student's road to becoming a licensed psychologist, for example, may be quite different from another graduate student's with the same goal. Since there are many different pathways that will lead you to successfully achieving your goals, the need to be flexible and make adjustments along the way should be anticipated and not viewed as problematic.

> *Since there are many different pathways that will lead you to successfully achieving your goals, the need to be flexible and make adjustments along the way should be anticipated and not viewed as problematic.*

Tips for Goal Setting

1. Take your time, utilizing self-awareness and reflection, when setting goals for yourself.
   - Assess your present academic, professional, and personal responsibilities and functioning (remember work-life balance!).
   - Reflect on the past—previous accomplishments, past goals, and former roadblocks—in reaching these goals.
   - Carefully and thoughtfully reflect on present goals and objectives.
   - Review your values statement—are your goals in line with the values you established?
   - Consider potential challenges to these present goals and objectives.
2. Utilize resources available to you.
   - Seek out help from mentors and advisors who can provide the following: assistance with drafting goals in line with your objectives; knowledge and experience of realistic

    timelines and steps involved in achieving your goals;
help with tracking your progress in attaining your goals;
assistance in reviewing the ongoing appropriateness
and relevance of your goals; knowledge of effective self-
care strategies while working to attain your goals; and
information to help you consider the relevance to your
present goals when deciding to pursue new opportunities.

- Network with seasoned professionals in your areas of
interest, inquiring about their own experiences, goals, and
paths to success.
- Seek guidance from upper-level peers in your graduate or
training programs who may share similar goals. They may
be particularly helpful in providing specific and realistic
steps needed to achieve these goals, and realistic timelines.

3. Reap the rewards.
   - Break larger and long-term goals into intermediate steps
   that can be measured and rewarded.
   - Remember to reward yourself appropriately each time a
   step or goal is achieved (e.g., a break to watch your favorite
   television show, a weekend off from your dissertation,
   dinner with friends). Not only is it well deserved, but it is
   necessary to help you re-energize and maintain a positive
   well-being for the remaining tasks ahead.

Flexibility, Adaptability, and Modifications

Once your goals are clearly identified and outlined, also remember that while consistency and commitment are key ingredients
for attaining goals, realistic goals are ones that are not set in stone.
Rather, goals are dynamic and may require alterations or changes
as your life and priorities change as well. Continue to review your
goals and maintain awareness of your priorities and the changes in
your personal and professional lives that can influence the progress
of attaining your goals. You will need to revisit and revaluate the
countless goals you may face as a graduate student over the course
of your training years. For example, you may need to reassess a goal
of accruing enough supervised hours at a training site for licensure
requirements if programmatic issues arise, such as your supervisor
leaving at your training site, or if you are dealing with unexpected

personal or family challenges. Remember, these are *your* goals. New experiences, changing interests, or other personal and professional factors that alter the balance in your life may result in modifying your goals as needed.

Continue to review your goals and maintain awareness of your priorities and the changes in your personal and professional lives that can influence the progress of attaining your goals.

Regularly monitor your progress to maintain flexibility within your goals. Because it would be impossible to anticipate every event and every bump along the road in graduate school (e.g., getting the flu and having to stay in bed for days, rushing home for a family member's illness or death, dealing with computer viruses or unexpected crashes), it is important that you remain flexible in your approach when it comes to working toward your goals.

While it is important to be self-disciplined to ensure that you progress toward your goals, being overly rigid about what is achieved and when may not be realistic and may prove counterproductive. Graduate students quickly learn that many things take longer than originally anticipated and nothing ever seems to go exactly according to plan. Failure to be flexible and adaptable may serve only to increase your stress and anxiety, which is unlikely to help you to achieve your goals. Make adjustments along the way, and respond to the feedback you pick up on from your own monitoring of your progress. For example, if after a week you have not been able to accomplish as much as you had hoped, modify your schedule the following week, allocating more time to work on achieving this goal and putting other desired activities temporarily on hold.

Time Management

One of the greatest challenges graduate students face is not having enough time. It is perhaps our most precious and limited resource. Graduate school can often feel like a continuous game of "Beat the Clock," with always more work to do than available time to complete it, in all areas of your life—academic, professional, and personal. How often have you felt the pressure to skip the gym or turn down an opportunity with friends or family while working to meet a pressing deadline? Time can therefore be a significant challenge to accomplishing your goals and managing self-care and psychological wellness.

Take Stock of Your Time

Whether it is a daily goal that may take only a few minutes to accomplish or a career goal that may take years to reach, budget and schedule your time accordingly in consideration of all other obligations and tasks in your personal and professional life. Once again, awareness is a critical primary step when it comes to tending to your own time management. Have you ever asked yourself where the time has gone when doing work? Try writing down how you spend each hour of the day for one week to obtain a clear picture. In reviewing this weekly schedule, consider how many hours per week are devoted to academic work, professional work, personal responsibilities, and self-care. Is there an imbalance in this schedule, with one area receiving too much attention and another not receiving enough? Are there parts of the day during which time has been wasted or used in a less effective manner?

You can apply this time assessment to consider your goals. Remember that you can consider goals in various areas of your life, beyond just the academic or professional, and can therefore extend to such examples as exercising, attending to spiritual needs, maintaining successful relationships, and so forth. A greater awareness of how you utilize your time, while also considering the various goals of your life, can be a positive first step in more effectively managing your time to work toward achieving these goals.

Voice of Experience: One Psychologist's Perspective

I have two memories from graduate school that remain vivid to this day. The first is sitting at my desk late one night studying, with my eyes glazing over and me not having any idea of what I was reading. I remember saying to myself that if only I needed just two or three hours of sleep per night, I could really do a great job as a graduate student. The second memory from graduate school is having a paper to write, and finding it difficult to motivate myself to sit down and get started on it. It was at that time that I decided that my laundry needed to be done and my kitchen cleaned and reorganized. Both memories highlight for me issues of time management, effective organization and planning, realistic goals, and activity prioritization by importance rather than preference.

Prioritize: A-B-C Lists

Additionally, prioritizing individual goals, tasks, and objectives can help you to utilize your time most effectively. Given that whatever assignment is due soonest will often demand your greatest focus, how do you then divide your time and attention so that you attend to the immediate and short-term goals while also continuing to make progress toward your long-term goals?

An A-B-C priority list is one helpful technique for prioritization. Priority lists, such as the A-B-C list, can help you organize and keep track of assignments, tasks, and goals to be completed. Additionally, since graduate students are always adding new things to the list, making it at times seem endless, the process of crossing items off your list after completing tasks enables you to develop realistic perspectives on what you have achieved. The A-B-C priority list includes three separate lists of tasks or goals.

The "A" list, meant for time-limited and essential tasks, often will involve tasks that must be completed that day. This is also known as the "must-do" list.

The "B" list incorporates important tasks that are to be accomplished within the week. Thus, while they are essential for assisting you in accomplishing your goals, they are less time-sensitive or urgent than the "A" list.

Finally, the "C" list, also known as the "nice-to-do" list, is for tasks or projects that you would like to attend to when the time is available.

Be sure to update your A-B-C priority list each day. Items left over from the day's "A" list can be moved to the top of the "A" list for the next day to ensure they are addressed. Additionally, as the week progresses, items from the "B" list may need to be moved up to the "A" list to continue to stay on top of your tasks, ensuring that they are completed on time. Furthermore, on the rare and blissful occasion that all items on your "A" list have been completed, there are a number of options to consider. You may choose to get a head start on tomorrow's action items and begin to attend to items on the "B" list that will be placed on tomorrow's "A" list. You may also decide to use this time to begin addressing an item on the "C" list. A third option is to use the time for self-care or to reward yourself for the work you achieved in completing the day's tasks, taking a break from work and enjoying the time off. Daily review of the day's accomplishments, tomorrow's goals and priorities, and how your list reflects those goals and priorities, can help you keep track of the goals you have achieved, the progress you are making toward other goals, and the goals that will continue to require your time and attention.

Additional Time Management Strategies

To better manage your time, find ways to combine tasks.[6] For example, combine exercise with social time by inviting friends to join you at the gym, or go to the library with peers and take periodic study breaks together. Listen to books on tape or recordings of class lectures while commuting to and from school or while on the treadmill.

Managing your time effectively as a graduate student also requires a considerable commitment to avoid distractions.[7] This may include choosing not to work in the student lounge area at school, where there may be ample opportunity to become distracted by peer conversations, and not logging on to the Internet when completing work to avoid temptations of browsing favorite blogs or social networking sites.

Take appropriate breaks, and allot time to rest.[8] Planning breaks ahead of time when a long period of work is anticipated, as well as setting a time limit for each break or rest, can help with time management and also help prevent procrastination. Break down work into manageable chunks, and schedule a 10-minute break every hour or after every two chapters you read. This can help to maintain focus and concentration in the long run. With all of these time management strategies, it is also important to keep in mind that moderation is key. Too much multitasking in an effort to manage your time can challenge your long-term self-care, balance, health, and wellness goals. Sometimes, just relaxing and enjoying yourself is important (and needed) too!

Sometimes the time management challenge comes when your work takes longer than originally budgeted, resulting in never reaching the bottom of that to-do list. Remember that your time is valuable, and it is important to treat it as such. Respect the boundaries of the time you have allotted for yourself to complete a task or accomplish a goal. One way of doing so is committing yourself to the decision that based on the amount of time you have allotted to complete a task, when the time is up, you will be done with the task.

Previously introduced in Chapter 5 as a technique for balancing the personal and professional demands of the graduate school lifestyle, setting time limits on academic tasks can also be an effective time management tool. For example, if I were to allot myself three hours to complete a take-home exam, at the end of those three hours I will accept the product I have completed, even if another half hour may help me earn an extra two points on the exam. Instead, I may choose to use that half hour as a break, or begin working on the next task on my list. Some graduate students have said they even set a timer to signal when their time is up for working on a particular task or when it is time to return to work after taking a break.

Focusing on the bigger picture, remembering your larger goals, and not getting locked in with tunnel vision on one task are key, yet can be challenging, particularly in the beginning of your grad school career. To ensure that larger goals are kept in view, take a few moments to reflect and ask yourself how the possible extra few points on the exam or paper fits within your larger goals of finding time for exercise, more sleep, or time with family.

Overcoming the Graduate Student Challenges to Goal Setting and Time Management

The lifestyle and common characteristics of graduate students can often make goal setting and time management strategies easier to discuss in theory than to actually put into practice. While setting goals and budgeting time sound highly beneficial, it can be difficult to begin putting such strategies into practice when each day is a whirlwind of tasks to complete one after the next. Adopting these strategies in many ways goes against the graduate student lifestyle and against the environment in which graduate students work and are taught. Thus, effective utilization of these practices requires more than simply beginning to keep a schedule or budgeting your time more effectively. Rather, it also involves a degree of personal consideration regarding what it means to be a successful graduate student. Take time to consider what being successful will mean to you in all facets of your life: as a graduate student, a friend, a romantic partner, a son or daughter, a community member. Each of these roles must be considered in your conceptualization of how you choose to uniquely define success.

The following are our recommendations for overcoming common challenges when it comes to goal setting and time management.

Redefine the "Perfect" Graduate Student

You have achieved your place in the graduate program after considerable hard work and determination. You may be among the many graduate students who believe they have to "do it all" when it comes to accomplishing tasks and taking advantage of opportunities during your time in school. Such students often set academic and professional goals that reflect this perfectionistic attitude, leaving little to no time for personal goals or self-care. Consider what it truly means to be a competent graduate student. Rather than clinging to the unrealistic expectation of being a "perfect" graduate student, consider viewing graduate school as an opportunity to learn not just from classes, internship, and practicum, but also from your mistakes.[9]

> Rather than clinging to the unrealistic expectation of being a "perfect" graduate student, consider viewing graduate school as an opportunity to learn not just from classes, internship, and practicum, but also from your mistakes.

Learn to Say "No"

This also means that you are not Superman or Superwoman. Recognize your limitations—every human being has them. While you may wish to "do it all," one of the most essential components of managing time and accomplishing goals lies in your ability to say "no." This is often a word that does not exist in the vocabulary of graduate students: individuals who do not want to disappoint or let down professors, supervisors, mentors, family, friends, and others. However, it is essential to recognize that you cannot do it all—too many good things is still too much and can negatively influence your efforts at self-care and impact your psychological wellness. Rather, learn to delegate tasks when possible, and make decisions about which opportunities to pursue and which ones to decline as essential self-care practice. While it may be tough, at times you may need to say "I would love to do that and thank you for the opportunity, but I am managing all I can right now and cannot take on anything else." This will enable you to be more present and devote greater attention to the tasks you have committed to, while also allowing time for self-care.

Understand that Graduate School Is a Marathon, Not a Sprint

At times you may become impatient with your phase of training, wishing to achieve your goals right now even though they realistically may take years to accomplish. As a result, you may attack these goals with a sprint-like pace, only to find yourself at risk for burnout. Setting goals and making progress toward your goals requires a steady marathon-like pace. Set a pace that you can maintain throughout your time in graduate school and professional career. Consider graduate school as a series of stages, with each stage having a different set of goals to work toward, and attend to one stage at a time.[10] These staged goals can reflect the developmental progression of your training and apply for academic, research, and clinical goals. This will allow you to have the energy and drive to continue to take the steps required to accomplish your longer term goals while also maintaining your psychological well-being.

One Student's Experience

When I (LC) first entered graduate school I was in awe of all the various activities and accomplishments of my peers ahead of me. These classmates held jobs in the field, attained positions in professional organizations, wrote research articles, served as teaching assistants and research assistants, presented at conferences, received awards, gained practicum experiences in particular niche areas of the field, and so much more. Each time I heard about another peer's activity or accomplishment, I would think to myself, "Oh, I have to do that," and furthermore believed that I had to accomplish it at that very moment! Other times I would think, "What's wrong with me that I have not yet achieved what that student has?"

Realistically, however, there were not enough hours in the day, and it did not make logical sense professionally to pursue all of these goals for myself. Furthermore, many of these students were years ahead of me in a program that I had just begun, and these lists of accomplishments were held by over a dozen peers, meaning that no single person could realistically ever accomplish all of them. Yet, in a desire to achieve it all and create that impressive C.V., I had lost sight of my own interests and passions within the field. Taking time to develop a smaller number of goals that reflected my own interests, I have over the last few years been able to pursue these goals with far greater depth than I had ever anticipated. It required me to take pride in the accomplishments of my classmates, yet not feel as though my classmates' goals also had to be mine just because we were in the same training program, or even shared similar career aspirations. Besides, how realistic is it to become a child/adolescent/adult/geropsychologist, researcher, practitioner, *and* professor?

Be Your Own Advocate

Managing others' demands and expectations of you is another piece to consider as it relates to goal setting and time management. Despite your best efforts to prioritize your own goals and to spend your time wisely, others may have expectations of you that can make it difficult to maintain the boundaries and goals you have set for yourself. Professors, peers, friends, family members, and others may not be aware of all of the demands on your time and energy. Be open with those close to you regarding the extent of your responsibilities and goals, and work to find ways to compromise when they need something from you. When expectations and demands far exceed your capacity, be an advocate for yourself, your goals, and your priorities.

Ben's Time Management: Beginning to Chart His Course

Ben's A-B-C Priority List

Here an example of an A-B-C priority list that Ben has created for himself. It reflects his obligations, hobbies, and some of the goals he has set for himself during his graduate training.

A List

- Class 8–10:30 a.m.
- Supervision @ 3 p.m.
- Finish research paper due tomorrow
- Call client to reschedule Thursday's appointment
- E-mail advisor about setting up meeting for selecting dissertation chairperson
- Exercise at the gym

B List

- Research articles for theories paper due Monday
- Complete research methods homework assignment due Thursday
- Make flyer for Grad Student Social Night
- Finish updating client treatment plans by Friday
- Buy groceries
- Pick up birthday gift for Lindsay

C List

- Begin researching internship sites
- Secure volunteer/service position
- Obtain a TA position within the next year
- Find a mentor
- Join a running club

Personal Values Statement

Personal values statements can help create the foundation for goal setting. Write a personal values statement that reflects your mission, values, and attitudes, reflecting on your roles as a graduate student as well as other personal and professional roles that are important for you. You may refer back to Ben's personal values statement, located earlier in this chapter, as an example.

Goal Setting Activity

Now that you have created your personal values statement, complete the following lists to begin brainstorming goals. Remember to develop goals that will reflect the values you expressed in your personal values statement.

Short-Term Goals

ACADEMIC

Goal	Steps Required to Accomplish	Possible Challenges	Realistic Deadline

PROFESSIONAL

Goal	Steps Required to Accomplish	Possible Challenges	Realistic Deadline

PERSONAL

Goal	Steps Required to Accomplish	Possible Challenges	Realistic Deadline

Long-Term Goals

ACADEMIC

Goal	Steps Required to Accomplish	Possible Challenges	Realistic Deadline

PROFESSIONAL

Goal	Steps Required to Accomplish	Possible Challenges	Realistic Deadline

PERSONAL

Goal	Steps Required to Accomplish	Possible Challenges	Realistic Deadline

Reflection Activity

Reflect on your specific goals regarding self-care and psychological wellness. To what extent have these goals been a priority in the past? What changes can you make to manage your time more effectively, and to more effectively balance all your goals—including self-care goals? What actions can you begin taking to incorporate and make progress toward these important goals?

8

Developing Your Self-Care Plan

Self-Care Does Exist?!

Natalia started her internship placement three months ago. While anticipating some challenges in her transition from graduate school to full-time clinical training, Natalia is surprised by just how difficult the adjustment has been, both personally and professionally. After weeks of hesitating to talk about this with anyone, fearing others will think she is unable to keep up with the demands of the 50- to 60-hour workweek, she decides to open up with her supervisor and discusses the rough transition of relocating and adjusting to the schedule, caseload, and demands of the training position. When her supervisor asks what Natalia is doing for self-care, Natalia is caught off guard. Self-care was never discussed in Natalia's graduate program, and she presumed it had no place in the highly demanding schedule of her training position. After meeting with her supervisor, Natalia begins to consider where to start and what self-care practices will be most beneficial and enjoyable for her. While self-care sounds like a great idea, she finds herself questioning just how this is going to fit into her life.

Self-Care What Does It Really Involve?

"Self-care is . . . a skillful attitude and a lifelong commitment." [1]

It is time to begin developing your own self-care plan! But what does the term *self-care* mean to you? Developing a personal and unique plan begins with understanding *all* that self-care encompasses. It is not uncommon to hear of self-care within the context of peers or professors reminding one another to find time to enjoy an upcoming weekend or dinner for the purpose of "self-care." However, self-care is much more than these one-time events. What self-care truly means is the ongoing practice of self-awareness and self-regulation for the purpose of balancing psychological, physical, and spiritual needs of the individual.[2] Self-care practices attend to your physical, emotional, relational, as well as spiritual or religious needs, and are integrated into your daily life on an ongoing basis.

> *Self-care practices attend to your physical, emotional, relational, as well as spiritual or religious needs, and are integrated into your daily life on an ongoing basis.*

Self-Care Is . . .

Self-awareness: ongoing observation and attunement to your experience, including risk factors and warning signs for challenges to psychological wellness (e.g., distress, problems with professional competence, burnout, secondary traumatic stress).

   Self-regulation: regular use of self-care practices and techniques integrated into your life.

Self-care is not an obligation or an act of indulgence. Practicing self-care is not selfish but, rather, essential to your role as a psychologist. Nor is it a one-time, monthly, or yearly activity we do in order to cross it off our to-do list. Rather, it is a continuously evolving process that changes as your personal and professional needs, demands, and experiences shift over the course of your life and career.[3] Therefore, self-care is different based on your individuality, life circumstances, and needs. Furthermore, self-care for you as a student will be somewhat different from your self-care needs as an early career psychologist, and different still as a more seasoned professional (although there likely will be some overlap).

Finally, keep in mind that the overall goal of self-care is always the promotion of your psychological wellness and effective functioning. As such, while commitment to practicing self-care is important, self-care is never meant to be another obligation, obstacle, or unenjoyable experience. Thus it is important to approach self-care with an attitude of patience, and to understand that it is not an all-or-nothing phenomenon. This way you can begin making small steps toward establishing self-care immediately that can develop over time into lasting and significant gains. Let us now begin to explore the many aspects of self-care.

Self-Care Practices

"Self-care is not a narcissistic luxury to be filled as time permits; it is a human requisite, a clinical necessity, and an ethical imperative."[4]

Biobehavioral Self-Care

Biobehavioral self-care involves attending to the physical needs and care of your body.[5] This includes maintaining adequate levels of sleep, nutrition, and exercise.[6] Consider how many hours you sleep per night on average. Feeling fatigued on a regular basis can make it extremely difficult to function effectively throughout the day. Developing a regular sleep schedule and getting enough sleep each night are important first steps in taking care of yourself and ensuring that you are then able to care for others in both your personal and professional lives.

Between hectic schedules and limited budgets, graduate students as a whole appear to have among the unhealthiest eating habits around. How often do you find yourself running from one obligation to the next, grabbing yet another caffeinated beverage or unhealthy meal (at times skipping meals all together)? Packing meals and snacks the night before to have with you throughout the day and blocking out mealtimes in your daily schedule can be helpful strategies when attending to your personal self-care needs.

Staying active benefits both the body and mind. Scheduling time for exercise, joining a young professionals sports league, exercising at the local gym, or just engaging in physical activity outdoors are all healthy ways of incorporating exercise into your life.

Pursuing regular medical and dental exams are also important for maintaining an overall healthy lifestyle.[7] While this may sound obvious, these appointments are often the first to be overlooked or forgotten in the onslaught of exams, meetings, classes, and your own clients' appointments.

Voice of Experience: One Psychologist's Perspective

I have found that while my self-care needs have changed throughout my career, and my self-care activities have changed at times, one thing has been a constant: exercise. Whenever I get too busy and start missing workouts, those closest to me can tell. They often ask whether something is wrong and, for those closest to me, why I am being so crabby? When my schedule becomes too busy it is often because I have overscheduled myself, saying "yes" to too many things. I still struggle with saying "no" and setting limits, I need to continually remind myself that too many good things is still too much, and I need to always be sure I make time for exercise in my schedule.

Relaxation, Enjoyment, and Fulfilling Activities

Participating in hobbies or activities that are relaxing or stress reducing for you are also essential components of your overall self-care plan. Such self-care practices can be considered as "healthy escapes" from the daily tasks of your personal and professional lives that at times may feel stressful, challenging, overwhelming, or perhaps even all-consuming.[8]

Like many of the self-care components, the effectiveness of these self-care practices is tied to your individual interests, lifestyle, and creativity. Remember, these activities are *never* meant to become additional sources of stress, and so selecting activities that are practical and enjoyable is key to assisting you in your ability to maintain your self-care plan. Below is a list to help you get started with some ideas, many of which were provided by graduate students. What all of these self-care activities have in common is that they are activities sought *not* for accomplishment or achievement. Keep in mind that many wonderful practices exist beyond this list because self-care is limited only by your imagination. See Chapter 10 for a glimpse into some of the more nontraditional and creative self-care practices enjoyed by fellow graduate students.

Remember, these activities are never meant to become additional sources of stress, and so selecting activities that are practical and enjoyable is key to assisting you in your ability to maintain your self-care plan.

- Journaling
- Engaging in daily relaxation practices such as meditation and yoga
- Doing crossword puzzles
- Reading
- Listening to or making music
- Going to a local farmer's market or other outdoor event on weekends
- Hosting a potluck dinner
- Creating art
- Walking your dog in the morning or evening
- Cooking
- Watching a favorite television show or movie

Relational Self-care

Another component of self-care is involvement in personal social relationships. Such relationships can include romantic partners, family, friends, and pets.[9] When it comes to relationships and self-care, the quality of these relationships—how meaningful you find them and how actively you engage in them—is more important than the quantity of relationships.[10] In regard to self-care, these relationships can provide the following:

- Refreshing perspectives beyond the scope of psychology and graduate school
- Opportunities to break away from your academic or professional work

- Needed social support
- Security, companionship, and stability[11]

How can you find time to nurture your personal relationships and attend to relational self-care in graduate school? While it will be important for you to consider your own specific relationships, needs, and opportunities to attend to this aspect of self-care, here are some examples:

- Actively plan for and take breaks away from your schoolwork to spend time with family or friends.
- Reserve a specific time each night to talk or videoconference with those who live far away from you.
- Schedule regular "date nights" or evenings with friends or significant others.
- Make dinner a special time in your day to catch up with those you care about.
- Acknowledge and enjoy coming home to and being greeted by a beloved pet.

Engaging in relational self-care requires you to take on an active role in establishing and maintaining your relationships. Do not wait for others to contact you or "make the first move" because the countless other professional and personal demands on your time can make it all too easy to place relationships on the back burner if you place the responsibility on others to establish or maintain them. Instead, actively pursue the important relationships in your life, no matter how busy or hectic your life may get at times, so that these relationships do not fade away.

Engaging in relational self-care requires you to take on an active role in establishing and maintaining your relationships.

Spiritual/Religious Self-Care

Spiritual and religious practices are yet another self-care outlet. Just as it is important to address your own physical, emotional, and relational self-care needs, it is also important to address various aspects of your spiritual self. Spirituality, a component of every individual, is similar to personality, and thus present but varied from one person to the next.[12] In general, spirituality can be viewed as developing a "sense of connection . . . with a force transcendent of one's self, such as nature, the universe, and/or God."[13] The concept of religion incorporates spirituality but also involves a search for identity, belongingness, or wellness carried out through rituals or behaviors recognized by a particular group or organization.[14] It is certainly possible to be spiritual without participating in any organized religion. There are a variety of spiritual or religious self-care practices, many of which are commonly practiced by today's psychologists as a form of self-care:

- Prayer or meditation and attending religious services have been found to be the most common religious or spiritual coping practices used in times of distress among psychologists who identified as religious.[15]
- Additionally, in a study of psychologist self-care strategies, 51.5% endorsed the practice of meditation or prayer and 33.8% endorsed attendance at church services.[16]
- Psychologists have also endorsed spiritual self-care through meditation, nature walks, and creation of meaning and purpose in one's life.[17]
- Daily mindfulness practice is also suggested as a positive self-care strategy for psychologists.[18]

Self-Care Practices in Your Professional Life

Often the irony of self-care is that we find ourselves practicing it when we have the most time available—typically during weekends or in the evenings after a long day of work or school. But practicing self-care during the hectic times is just as important and an essential component of your overall self-care lifestyle. Take some time to consider what areas of your professional life are most in need of self-care practices as you begin to read on.

You may feel that you have little control over academic and professional demands at this time in your training. Maintaining some degree of control over your work schedule, such as through time management practices (see Chapter 7), is one professional self-care practice that can help. Here is a list of additional professional self-care strategies to consider as you begin to create a self-care plan:

- Establish appropriate limits and boundaries with your school- and professional work.
- Create realistic expectations to help maintain a degree of control over your work and reduce the likelihood of problems with professional competence.[19]
- Schedule breaks in your day.
- Maintain a manageable caseload.
- Take periodic vacations.[20]
- Schedule into your calendar administrative time for documentation between clients, and avoid, when possible, scheduling multiple clients back to back throughout the day.
- Reserve time for lunch, which can frequently be forgotten or rushed.

Graduate students often do not have direct control over their caseloads, but this does not mean you should be passive about it. Maintaining some degree of control over your caseload for the purpose of self-care can include keeping supervisors informed about your caseload in terms of both quantity and content. You should not assume that your supervisors are aware of your workload and that they are thinking about your self-care. Keep supervisors informed of the composition of your caseload (e.g., multiple concurrent suicidal clients) and its size (e.g., four new referrals in the past several days).

Although the money and time required to take vacations may seem nonexistent during graduate school, even small overnight trips, weekend camping trips, or visiting friends or family during time off from school can be ways to incorporate affordable vacations into the graduate student lifestyle. Try taking advantage of last-minute online travel bargains. You may also consider volunteer work, a self-care practice among 40% of surveyed psychotherapists, as an outlet from work-related activities.[21] Taking time for vacations or activities with family and friends to help maintain balance was among the top 10 strategies psychotherapists identified as contributing to their well-functioning.[22] More recent research has revealed that taking vacations and scheduling breaks throughout one's workday were found to be two of the seven highest-ranked coping strategies endorsed by surveyed psychologists.[23]

One Student's Experience

At my (LC) very first practicum site, appointment scheduling was handled by office staff and clinicians were required to routinely update weekly calendars to indicate daily and weekly availability. Wanting to maximize my availability in the hopes of being able to work with many clients, I found myself having days filled with supervision, meetings, and psychotherapy appointments back to back from morning until early evening. By the last psychotherapy appointment I would often be hungry, tired, and dreading the day's worth of treatment notes waiting to be written. One day I realized that despite the fact that scheduling was handled by my practicum site, I had failed to recognize the degree of control I did have over my schedule. I began blocking out an hour break in the middle of my day to use for lunch and to start writing treatment notes from morning sessions. Rather than it being a "waste of time" as I had feared, it was both highly productive and also beneficial, providing me with a much needed energy boost to carry me through the remainder of the day.

Personal Psychotherapy

Personal psychotherapy can serve as a valuable self-care strategy of both preventive and reparative means for both the personal and professional stresses and challenges you will experience in graduate school. Approximately 70–74% of psychology graduate students surveyed have received psychotherapy treatment at some point prior to or during graduate school.[24] The most commonly cited reasons for seeking psychotherapy while in graduate school include the following:

Personal psychotherapy can serve as a valuable self-care strategy of both preventive and reparative means for both the personal and professional stresses and challenges you will experience in graduate school.

- Personal growth
- Desire to improve as a clinician

- Adjustment or developmental issues
- Depression[25]

The cost of psychotherapy, the time commitment involved, and confidentiality issues are three considerable obstacles for a graduate student interested in entering psychotherapy.[26] Consider inquiring about sliding fee scales from local practitioners. Additionally, many graduate programs maintain lists of graduates of their program who are now licensed and willing to provide psychotherapy to students at a reduced rate. If your program does not maintain such a list, consider speaking with your program director about creating this important resource for yourself and other students.

Personal psychotherapy for a graduate student clinician can improve emotional functioning, reduce the emotional stresses and burdens that naturally exist in the practice of psychotherapy, and provide a greater awareness and understanding of the client's role and perspective in psychotherapy.[27] This can be of particular benefit during your time as a student, in the earlier stages of developing your therapeutic and counseling skills and adjusting to this new role as psychologist in training. Psychotherapy can also help you address personal issues, such as taking care of an ill parent, and professional issues, such as dealing with a client's suicide attempt, that if not addressed could contribute to compromised objectivity and judgment or other compromised abilities.[28]

Graduate students with histories of trauma can utilize psychotherapy as a self-care practice to address their past experiences, which can help to reduce the risk of secondary traumatic stress and increase competence in working with trauma populations.[29] Greater self-awareness and self-understanding, an increase in self-esteem or self-confidence, improved relationships, personal growth, and improvement in therapeutic skills and abilities have also been reported benefits among psychotherapists who have sought out personal psychotherapy.[30] As a psychologist in training, these benefits can be of incredible value to you—and your clients!

Tips for Developing Your Self-Care Plan

1. Review your past and present self-care history.
   - To what extent, if any, are you already practicing self-care?

- What activities do you already engage in that can be considered self-care?
- How often do you participate in such activities?

2. Select which areas of self-care (physical, emotional, relational, spiritual/religious, professional) you will begin to focus on in your plan.
   - Don't aim for perfection.
     - Keep in mind that it is impossible to attend to all areas of self-care perfectly.
   - Consider what areas of self-care require the most attention, are the most important to you, or have been the most neglected, to assist you in beginning your self-care plan.

3. Personalize your self-care plan.
   - Be creative.
     - Consider self-care strategies unique to your needs and interests—find what is relaxing, rejuvenating, and enjoyable for you.
   - Be open to changes.
     - Continually review your plan and be open to amending it and trying new strategies as needed.

4. Put the plan into action.
   - Start small.
     - Begin putting your plan into action with small, more manageable self-care practices or changes in your life (e.g., a weekly walk with your partner, eating a healthy breakfast every morning, ending each day with a five-minute mindfulness exercise).
   - Don't give up!
     - Remember that setbacks are common when beginning a self-care regimen. Do not be tempted to throw away your hard work and dedication after an occasional misstep.

Some Final Thoughts on Self-Care

As you begin to consider the self-care practices you currently engage in and those that you plan to incorporate, keep in mind that not all self-care practices are positive. At times, often without even fully recognizing it, you may engage in efforts to alleviate distress that have resulted in utilizing maladaptive self-care practices. Maladaptive self-care strategies include the following:

- Self-medicating with alcohol, drugs, or food[31]
- Ignoring needs for adequate levels of sleep and exercise[32]
- Neglecting to set limits out of the fear of being seen as uncooperative or not a team player
- Treating yourself to items you cannot afford
- Making poor attempts at balance and not engaging in occasional pleasurable activities[33]
- Engaging in workaholic behavior to get through challenges or issues (e.g., taking fewer vacations, skipping breaks in the workday, working longer hours, scheduling difficult clients or projects in succession)[34]
- Using clients to gain emotional support (e.g., engaging in inappropriate self-disclosure, spending more time with certain clients than others)[35]

Maladaptive self-care practices can have significant implications for your personal health and well-being as well as for your professional competence and well-functioning. Graduate students at risk for developing vicarious traumatization need to be especially aware of maladaptive self-care practices such as excessive shopping, drinking, overeating, or avoiding friends.[36] As you progress in the early phase of your career, working to pay off student loans and establish yourself professionally, keep in mind that this is when you may be especially at risk for developing workaholic self-care behavior.[37]

Even positive activities can become problematic or maladaptive when done to excess. Moderation is the key when it comes to self-care. It is not that you should never drink alcohol or never eat ice cream if you enjoy them, but too much of a good thing is still too much. Similarly, engaging in positive self-care activities with the attitude of continually needing to improve, such as exercising many hours each day at the cost of having little to no other personal time, can turn a seemingly positive self-care practice into a maladaptive one. Do not allow "self-care" to become a rationalization for over-indulging in positive activities that may result in greater harm than help. Rather, work to continually self-assess and strive for balance in your life. This balance will be imperfect and ever changing, but any efforts to address it will likely be helpful.

Natalia's Self-Care Action Plan

Physical Self-Care

– Take dog for run Sunday mornings with friend Sarah.
– Pack healthy snacks (avoid the daily 3 p.m. vending machine raid).
– Reduce caffeinated beverages from five to three each day.

Emotional Self-Care

– Research local psychotherapists with sliding scale and Saturday a.m. appointment times.

Relational Self-Care

– Take dog for run Sunday mornings with friend Sarah.
– Each lunch with other interns instead of alone in my office.

Spiritual/Religious Self-Care

– Wake up 10 minutes earlier each morning and practice mindfulness.

Professional Self-Care

– Review caseload schedule, and make adjustments to limit the number of difficult clients back to back.
– Block out 2:00–2:30 p.m. in my calendar each day for lunch and catching up on e-mails.
– Try to leave the office by 6 p.m. each Friday.
– Continue to discuss self-care progress with my supervisor.

First self-care areas I want to focus on: emotional and professional.

The Do's and Don'ts of Effective Self-Care

Do . . .

• Engage in activities that are enjoyable.
• Incorporate self-care both within and outside of your professional and academic life.
• Partake in positive self-care activities that promote wellness.
• Consider the whole person (physical, emotional, relational, spiritual/religious, and professional) when it comes to self-care.

- Approach self-care with moderation—even too much self-care can be harmful.
- Remember that self-care is not all or nothing. Begin by taking small steps, and maintain reasonable and realistic expectations of yourself.
- Appreciate that self-care is not about being great or an expert at a given activity, but about how it makes you feel.
- Actively incorporate self-care into your life (develop a realistic plan, schedule time for self-care, etc.).
- Consider ways in which you can participate in self-care activities that address multiple aspects of self-care needs simultaneously.
- Talk with peers, colleagues, professors, and professionals to get ideas regarding self-care practices and support for your plan.
- Keep in mind that self-care is not a one-size-fits-all model.

Don't . . .

- Engage in maladaptive or harmful self-care activities.
- Consider self-care a luxury or unattainable goal for graduate students.
- Set yourself up for failure by trying to achieve perfect self-care practices overnight, taking on more than you can reasonably be expected to maintain over time.
- Compare your self-care practices to another's—remember that self-care is unique and specific to each individual.
- Assume that stress will resolve on its own or believe that self-care is needed only when you are experiencing significant consequences from your stress.

Developing a Self-Care Action Plan

STEP 1: REVIEW YOUR CURRENT SELF-CARE
PRACTICES AND STRATEGIES

On the following checklist of positive self-care behaviors, check off any and all behaviors that you currently engage in. Also include how often you engage in this activity.

_____ I take regularly scheduled breaks when doing academic work and professional work _____ % of the time.

_____ I take vacations periodically and *don't* bring work with me _____ % of the time.

_____ I have friends, hobbies, and interests unrelated to work and regularly engage in such related activities _____ % of the time.

_____ I exercise regularly, have a healthy diet, and maintain an appropriate weight _____ % of the time.

_____ I limit my work hours and caseload _____ % of the time.

_____ I participate in peer support, clinical supervision, and personal psychotherapy as preventive strategies _____ % of the time.

_____ I attend to my religious and spiritual side _____ % of the time.

_____ I regularly participate in relaxing activities (e.g., meditation, yoga, reading, music) _____ % of the time.

_____ I regularly participate in activities that I enjoy and look forward to _____ % of the time.[38]

Reflection Activity

Consider the number of items you checked off in the previous checklist. To what extent do you think you are currently attending to your psychological wellness through self-care?

What areas of self-care are you currently not attending to?

What maladaptive self-care practices are you currently engaging in?

STEP 2: DEVELOP A SELF-CARE ACTION PLAN

Now that you have assessed your current self-care behaviors, use the following list to brainstorm realistic self-care activities that you can begin incorporating into your overall self-care lifestyle today!

My self-care action plan:

Physical Self-Care

1.

2.

3.

Emotional Self-Care

1.

2.

3.

Relational Self-Care

1.

2.

3.

Spiritual/Religious Self-Care

1.

2.

3.

Professional Self-Care

1.

2.

3.

Ready, Set, Go!

Getting Started with Self-Care Now

Self-Care: Nice in Theory, Impossible in Practice?

Derek is a graduate student who has been feeling increasingly stressed and overworked over the last several months. But he has become motivated to begin a self-care plan after attending a presentation on self-care for graduate students. Eager to get a jump-start on self-care and wanting to make sure he does it "right," he creates a self-care plan that includes exercising daily, spending more time with family, attending weekly personal psychotherapy, finding a mentor, and joining a volunteer service group. After three weeks of attempting to follow his self-care plan, Derek is exhausted and behind in his schoolwork. He feels that he often fails to uphold his self-care plan on certain days in order to meet all of his other obligations or is exhausted by the end of the night after trying to do it all. He thought that self-care was supposed to help him better manage his workload, and now he feels that his attempt at self-care has proven that self-care is impossible and impractical for a graduate student.

Turning Your Plan into Reality

Now that you have created your self-care action plan in Chapter 8, you are all set to go out and live a fully balanced life. Problem solved, right? Well, not exactly. Perhaps as you developed your self-care plan you were wondering how you would actually go about incorporating these self-care practices into your life. If you are unfamiliar with self-care, it can seem to be a conundrum—practices that are supposed to make you feel more balanced and less stressed require time and attention from your already busy schedule, leaving self-care a goal that seems nice in theory, but impossible in practice.

Finding ways to actually incorporate self-care into your already hectic life without it becoming an additional burden is a particular challenge for graduate students. In graduate school, you are expected to read for every class, do every assignment well and hand it in on time, work with clients, conduct research, make money, maintain a social life and relationships with family and friends, *and* practice good self-care.[1] Often, you may switch from task to task multiple times in just one day. How can you realistically and helpfully begin to put your self-care action plan into practice?

> *Finding ways to actually incorporate self-care into your already hectic life without it becoming an additional burden is a particular challenge for graduate students.*

Boundaries, Limits, and Just Saying "No"

It is not uncommon to look from your weekly calendar to your self-care action plan and wonder where you will find the time to practice self-care, let alone finish everything on the weekly calendar! Likely this is because many of your professional and personal roles impose obligations and requirements, involving your time, commitment, and attention. However, consider the extent to which you have some control over the boundaries of these obligations. Establishing boundaries is one helpful and effective way of beginning to incorporate and practice self-care regimens into your life.

At first glance, it may seem that the environment of graduate school creates rigid and limiting boundaries. You are expected to attend this meeting, do that assignment, meet with this professor, and so on, making it feel at times that almost every hour of your day is controlled by your graduate school obligations. But consider the extent to which these boundaries are solid versus flexible.[2] While some requirements and obligations are certainly imposed boundaries, often you may have some flexibility within these boundaries. Boundaries, rather than serving as limitations on your life, can actually enable you to experience freedom and flexibility.[3]

The graduate school lifestyle has the potential to become all-consuming. At times it can be difficult to remember that while your educational career is valuable, you are more than just a graduate student. Are there times when you may have neglected your non-graduate student roles or allowed your graduate student role to spread into other areas of your life? Creating boundaries and setting limits for yourself can help prevent you from becoming the 24/7 graduate student, help to minimize the risk of distress and burnout, and allow you to work to maintain a more balanced and healthy lifestyle.

Making a commitment to establish boundaries and set limits in order to obtain more freedom and flexibility and practice self-care involves a shift in how you think about and approach your work and obligations. While graduate students often feel as though they have to give 100% of themselves in everything they do, it is typically both unrealistic and draining to put your best and fullest effort into everything that you do. Prioritizing tasks is an effective way of working to balance ongoing demands and self-care.

Reducing the "I musts" and "I shoulds," beginning to say "no" when appropriate, and recognizing when things are "good enough" are all ways of establishing realistic and healthy boundaries and limits for yourself.[4] For example, are you able to walk away from a project when it is "good enough" so that you can make it to a friend's birthday dinner on time and enjoy a few hours away from your work? Adopting a "good enough" mindset does not mean lowering your personal or professional standards or producing substandard work. What it does mean is assessing and recognizing the degree of contribution your time and energy will likely produce. An example that we have referred to a number of times already in this handbook is that of working all evening on a project and now being faced with a decision: Do you spend an additional two hours of work to potentially boost the project's quality from an A− to an A, or do you use that time for catching up on other work or engaging in self-care activities? It is up to you to decide whether the additional two hours spent on this project, hours that could be used for personal time or other professional obligations or work, is worth it for you.

Reflecting on and asking yourself whether forgoing self-care activities is worth the difference between the A– or the A on a project, in this example, is an important question when making efforts to incorporate self-care into your life. It is also important to keep in mind that such practices as saying "no" and setting limits are not limited to your academic work. In order to maintain a degree of control over your life and find ways to effectively and realistically practice self-care, be mindful to also establish healthy and realistic boundaries with clients and with those in your personal life as well.[5]

Boundary- and Limit-Setting Tips
- Assess and consider the rigidity versus flexibility of tasks and roles.
- Set time limits.
- Disconnect to reconnect. Designate time for yourself or with others when you will not check or answer texts or e-mails.
- Value your free time. A blank space in your calendar does not always have to be filled with school or other professional obligations.
- Assess and determine the level of effort and commitment you will give for each task and responsibility, keeping in mind that you cannot give 100% effort to everything.
- Before starting a project or task, ask yourself what the finished product or goal is, and consider, at times, the notion of doing a "good enough" job to make time for balance.
- Allow yourself to say "no." Remember that being a graduate student is not a 24/7 role.

Voice of Experience: One Psychologist's Perspective

It often feels like I can never complete my to-do list. As soon as I get close to the end of it, more tasks arise. In fact, I've come to expect this. I may have a report to review, a dissertation chapter to read and edit, a letter of recommendation to write, papers to grade, and so much more. I've learned that the inflow of work to be done is never-ending. That is not what I can control. But what I can control is when I check my e-mails and what time periods I set aside for self-care activities. I've learned to schedule periods when I will keep my computer turned off, won't check my e-mail, and will engage in self-care activities, family time, or just downtime. I have found that if I don't schedule these times they won't happen. I have to value self-care and make it a priority. So I schedule self-care time (usually) and keep that computer turned off (usually). After all, the work will be there waiting for me when I return (much more refreshed and better able to do the work).

Self-Care: All or Nothing?

Like Derek, many people approach self-care with an all-or-nothing attitude. If self-care is supposed to be good for us, why not try to do it all and engage in as many self-care practices as possible? It is important to be aware, however, that the personality characteristics that helped you succeed in college and gain acceptance to graduate school may interfere with effectively integrating self-care into your life. Having a Type A personality, although helpful at times in being productive and achieving goals, can make it challenging for you to recognize the need for and then the incorporation of self-care into your life. Additionally, common graduate student strengths—such as attention to detail, hard work, competitiveness, and overachievement—likely will not serve you well in integrating self-care into your life. You may find, as Derek discovered, that such qualities can also contribute to overachievement in self-care, that there can be such a thing as too much self-care to the point where it no longer becomes effective at positively contributing to our psychological wellness.

At the beginning, keep in mind that self-care is a lifelong and continuously evolving process that will need to adapt to the changes throughout the course of your personal life and professional career.[6] Currently, you are a "work in progress" when it comes to achieving ideal or aspirational professional goals related to the incorporation and practice of self-care.[7] Therefore, approaching self-care not as an all-or-nothing phenomenon, but as a process that will continuously be reviewed and modified in response to the changes that occur in your life, is more realistic.

It is impossible to expect to successfully carry out your self-care action plan to the fullest overnight or to be able to practice every element of self-care at all times, while also being a perfect graduate student, perfect clinician, perfect friend, perfect partner, and perfect family member. All psychotherapists, and this includes all graduate students as well, are human.[8] Therefore, to expect to be superhuman in any area of your life, including self-care, is unrealistic. You are not going to be able to earn the perfect grade on every assignment, and be the best clinician, and work extra hours at your side jobs, and conduct the most groundbreaking research, while also simultaneously implementing your self-care action plan perfectly.

Furthermore, as a work in progress, you do not need to be able to accomplish it all at one time. This may mean choosing to pursue two or three goals rather than trying to excel at six or seven at one time. Or it may mean saying "no" to some great opportunities, perhaps choosing not to present at an upcoming conference or accept a professor's invitation to participate in an extra research project or coauthor a paper together, in order to more effectively focus on other goals and also leave time for self-care. Saying "no" or deciding not to pursue a particular endeavor at the present moment may feel like you are giving up or that the opportunity is lost forever. Consider ways in which you may work to overcome the naturally occurring fear that by declining opportunities you will not be presented with such opportunities or asked again in the future. Keep in mind that your positive qualities that led people to offer you these opportunities will not disappear and others will see and value them in the future as well. Thus, while you cannot successfully and healthily do it all and do it all at once, you can do your best to work to achieve balance in the many roles you play and begin to incorporate self-care into your life, with the understanding that it is an evolving process in which even the smallest of steps you take can make powerful and important changes in your life.

I'll Start Tomorrow . . . or Maybe the Next Day

You now have your self-care action plan and are beginning to recognize ways in which you can successfully find the time and energy to incorporate self-care into your life. When do you start? Oftentimes, graduate students hold out for opportune moments to begin practicing self-care. Yet, "unfortunately, it is so easy to plan to begin practicing self-care after comprehensive exams, after the dissertation is defended, after internship, after licensure, and so on."[9]

So, when is the best time to start practicing self-care? Today! In reality, there is no optimal starting time for the practice of self-care. There will always be some challenges or demands in your personal and professional life that can make practicing self-care difficult. However, promoting psychological and emotional wellness in your life cannot wait. Review your self-care action plan, and choose one component that you can begin to address today to begin your path toward practicing a self-care regimen. Again, the goal is not to be practicing self-care perfectly all the time, but to begin incorporating self-care into your life to promote a balanced and healthy well-being. Any amount of self-care is better than no self-care at all.

The goal is not to be practicing self-care perfectly all the time, but to begin incorporating self-care into your life to promote a balanced and healthy well-being.

One Student's Experience

The following passage is from an early career psychologist reflecting on her efforts to balance graduate school and family during graduate school:

> *As a wife, mother, and type-A graduate student, I have a lot on my plate. Thus, I learned balance early to maintain quality work as a student and quality time with family. In the first semester of graduate school I worked very hard and received excellent grades. However, I was unhappy with the pace of my life. I did not have any time for myself or my husband and was constantly in a physical state of stress. It was in December of that semester that my husband suggested I not do any schoolwork during the weeknights, and instead focus on getting ready for school the next day and relaxing. It was a novel idea, and I gave it a try. This revolutionized my approach to graduate school. I quickly realized that the quality of my work was the*

same and I was much happier. When I allowed myself the time I needed to unwind and spend time with my husband, I was more energized, focused, and efficient when I sat down to work. I began to put time limits on schoolwork and just get done what I could in that time frame. My grades were the best they ever were. I learned to rest hard and work hard. When it was time to be serious, I was focused and efficient. And, when it was time to rest, I would forget about my responsibilities and be completely present with my family. This rhythm was so smooth, that we decided it was a good time to try for a baby. Our daughter was born in my fourth year of graduate school and I will admit, I did not return emails and phone calls as fast as I used to, but I felt I was able to do a sufficient job with my school responsibilities and thoroughly enjoyed my life with my family. Allowing myself to accept a new standard was difficult, but that permission freed me to be a great mom, a great wife, and still a great student. For me, self-care is essential to maintaining happiness in my relationships and quality in my work.

Finding Balance in an Imperfect World

Derek's initial attempts to do everything in his overly ambitious self-care plan resulted in feelings of frustration, inadequacy, and failure. These are definitely not the desired outcomes of practicing self-care. After reflecting on his self-care needs and how they might fit into his life with all his other ongoing requirements and demands on his time, Derek developed a much more realistic self-care plan. With the assistance of one of his faculty members, Derek prioritized his self-care activities. Derek decided that regular exercise was vital for his health and for maintaining his sanity during graduate school. But, rather than requiring himself to exercise 2 hours every day, Derek planned to exercise 45 to 60 minutes three or four times each week. Derek also decided that a weekly personal psychotherapy session was an important investment in his own well-being and would be time well spent. While regular community service involvement is important to Derek, he realized that he cannot do it all and that when he over-schedules himself he becomes stressed and overwhelmed.

Derek also wants to spend more time with his family, but their visit requests come at unpredictable times that often coincide with his work deadlines. So Derek has arranged to do a monthly community service activity with his family, setting 1 day per month for this. While Derek will still need to be flexible in response to changes in his responsibilities and work demands, he seems on his way to establishing a realistic and sustainable self-care plan.

"Top Ten Self-Care Lessons I Learned as a Graduate Student"

Beginning to practice and incorporate self-care is an ever-evolving process. As a graduate student and throughout your professional career, you will continue to use trial and error as you assess and adjust to the needs and challenges of your life. Here, graduate students share their insights, struggles, and lessons learned along the way in practicing self-care during the course of their graduate careers:

1. "Cleaning out all my kitchen cabinets and scrubbing the floors is not a good thing to do when I have a paper due tomorrow, no matter how much I would prefer to avoid working on that paper."
2. "Somehow, the work always gets done. I never regret the few hours I walked away from my work to take a break and relax."
3. "I learned that stress eating is not the best self-care option, because you'll end up with no energy from the sugar crash and extra pounds."
4. "Create a realistic morning routine that you enjoy. Plan something for yourself prior to checking your e-mail each day, and do it no matter what else you have planned that day."
5. "Spending the whole day not doing schoolwork, because I just need a break, often leaves me feeling more anxious than if I had just worked on something for a few hours and then spent the rest of the day to myself."
6. "Signing up for a race is great self-care to add extra motivation and incentive to head to the gym. It keeps me accountable, sane, and helps ensure my pants fit all year long!"
7. "I make eating three meals a day a priority. It sounds easy enough, but when I first started graduate school it was so easy to skip a meal because of the busy schedule."

8. "Self-care is really important but it also is a great excuse for procrastination. Learn for yourself the difference between when something is self-care and when something is just plain procrastination!"

9. "Never underestimate the power of a brief phone call with the right friend or family member to help you through a rough day."

10. "Sometimes professors are not the best models of self-care."

Recognizing Challenges and Establishing Boundaries Activity

Using the chart provided, list some of the challenges you anticipate or are experiencing as you begin to implement your self-care action plan. Then, after each challenge, provide one potential (and realistic) way of addressing this challenge to help you more successfully incorporate and practice your self-care techniques.

Challenge	Potential Solution

Reflection Activity

Review the self-care action plan you created in Chapter 8. Use this space to reflect on what will be your first step in beginning to implement this plan. What self-care practice will you begin to engage in first? Why? When will you begin? Continue to return to this space to journal and reflect on your self-care progress throughout the coming days and weeks.

Self-Care Prioritization List Activity

After reflecting on your self-care action plan, develop a prioritization list of your self-care activities. It is important to have self-care practices that vary in their degree of involvement and commitment, some taking just a few moments out of your day and others involving much greater amounts of time or requiring pre-reserved time to complete. Be sure to include in your list self-care practices that involve both smaller and larger levels of time and commitment.

MY SELF-CARE PRIORITIZATION LIST

An Inside Look at Self-Care Practices of Graduate Students

O VER THE LAST TWO CHAPTERS, YOU HAVE BEGUN LAYING THE foundation for establishing a lifestyle of self-care as you have reflected on, developed ideas for, and begun to plan ways in which self-care can and will be incorporated into your life as a graduate student. Perhaps one of the most fascinating things about self-care is the degree of individuality and creativity it allows for. When considering what may serve as a positive self-care activity for you, the key lies in finding the activities that are most enjoyable, relaxing, or replenishing for *you*, which for some graduate students, has led to discovering self-care activities that may be considered outside the box.

The following are descriptions from several graduate students reflecting on their own journeys toward beginning and continuing to engage in unique self-care practices. You will read about a wide range of activities that share a common thread: the important and vital role these activities serve within the lives of these graduate students. In reading these stories, take some time to consider what self-care activities you enjoy that may be considered outside the bounds of the more traditional or common self-care practices. As these graduate students remind us, the sky is the limit when it comes to positive self-care practices!

Perhaps one of the most fascinating things about self-care is the degree of individuality and creativity it allows for.

Playing Guitar—Douglas M. Girard

I have been playing guitar for about 13 years now. I bought my first guitar on my 16th birthday and have been hooked ever since. Nowadays, I don't have nearly as much time to play as I used to, but I still probably pick it up three or four times per week, usually for about an hour at a time. At first, playing guitar requires patience more than anything else. As a beginner, it can be very frustrating. I don't know if most people would even consider it to be a "self-care" activity at that stage. Often, it's not even much fun. But after a while, however, things change. At some point, that boundary between you, the guitar, and the music breaks down. Any musician who has been playing for a significant period of time will tell you that playing has some magical, soothing properties. Music can really help get you in touch with what you are feeling. Music connects us with those emotions that we are often too busy to notice. Other times, I think it can resonate with complex situations and emotions which are hard to relate to verbally or otherwise. Music, and particularly playing, can also expand emotions outward.

At the mature stage of playing, however, I don't think anyone would argue with the contention that playing has a considerable capacity for "self-care." My advice to people who are just picking up the guitar or any instrument seriously, is to be patient. Spend time playing with others and have fun with it. Eventually you will come to find your soul in it. For me playing guitar is therapeutic. It puts me in touch with my emotions and helps me to release them. It connects the mind and the body, which, at least for me, often unknowingly get out of sync. It also gets me out playing with other people. But when I play, I don't think about any of this. I just play.

Crafts and Scrapbooking—Catherine Ruscitti

I really enjoy crafting and scrapbooking and have for about 9 years. I try to do something creative, whether it be painting, drawing, scrapbooking, or creating some other craft, twice a month. However, if it's near a holiday or birthday, I usually do it more often because I enjoy adding personal touches to gifts via crafting.

I first started scrapbooking when I was 15 after going to a scrapbooking party with my mom. I have been scrapbooking ever since. As for crafting, this interest blossomed for me as an extension of scrapbooking as I started experimenting with different creative outlets. Painting, drawing, creating shadow boxes, and making collages are just some of the crafting activities that I really enjoy. Scrapbooking and crafting help me to calm down and clear my mind. It is probably the only time schoolwork or my clinical work isn't on my mind. I love being creative and enjoy incorporating my creativity into gifts for my friends and family by making framed collages, shadow boxes, or scrapbooks for them. It's relaxing and a great creative outlet that I can practice at home.

There are many kinds of classes that you can take to get ideas and improve your skills through art stores. Scrapbooking and crafting can be expensive, especially when starting out, in order to begin accumulating a collection of stickers, paper, albums, paints, tape, glitter, and pictures. It also requires creativity and patience. But, the memories you can create and share through scrapbooking and other crafts are worth it!

Fencing—Jon Gorman

My self-care activity is fencing. I began fencing at a fencing club when I was in high school. When I came to grad school, I looked into a few clubs in the area, and at one club the head coach offered to allow me to train there for free if I would teach a few classes per week in return. I'm typically at the club 1 or 2 days during the week, Saturday mornings, and occasionally I go to competitions on weekends.

If you want to begin fencing, you pretty much need to start with a group class or individual lessons. Many colleges/universities offer an introduction to fencing group class that lasts a few weeks. If not, there are fencing clubs all over the country that offer beginners classes. Many also offer beginners classes just for adults so it's not you with a bunch of 7-year-olds. Aside from the cost of the class itself, fencing equipment can be a bit pricey. However, most clubs have equipment that members can freely borrow at any time. One of the nice things about fencing is that it is a sport for people of any age. Tournaments are classified by ability and by age, so whether it's your first time or you're 65 years old, you'll be able to find a tournament that is within your ability level. There is even wheelchair fencing!

I really enjoy fencing. I've seen it described as "physical chess," and that epithet definitely holds true. Fencing is great exercise and a sport that requires a lot of strategy. Like any other individual sport, how you do is completely up to you, so I like the accountability . . . it keeps you humble. Something I've discovered through fencing is the power of one's mind to influence an outcome. When I am fencing, if in my mind I am the slightest bit under-confident, over-confident, inflexible, anxious, constricted, or distracted from the present moment, I won't do my best. As a result, it is as important to practice and develop mental discipline, focus, and openness under stressful situations as it is to practice techniques and stay physically fit. I've also discovered that the same is true with just about any other pursuit in life. I try to approach my psychotherapy clients with the same exact attitude (minus the part about trying to stab them with a sword as fast as possible)!

Community Service—Jueta McCutchan

I was first acquainted with the notion of social justice during my undergraduate studies where traditions of service and justice were highly emphasized. Through my first experience I learned a great deal about the power of the human spirit to persevere through so much adversity and the consequences for those who do not or cannot do so. Since this first experience, I sought out other opportunities, usually through various service organizations at my undergraduate and now graduate campuses. I attempt to volunteer at least once per week or at least 4 to 5 hours per month. I figure an hour per week is something that everyone can do, and it's a great way to keep me motivated for the entire month.

As for the advice I would provide to anyone wanting to start volunteering, I would tell them to first think about what they truly like to do to give back. The things that I have enjoyed will not necessarily be the things that others enjoy and vice versa. Once they figure out what they truly enjoy, [they should] go online and talk to others about potential opportunities. Organizations are always looking for a few good people.

Volunteering affords me the opportunity to meet and converse with people from all walks of life. Oftentimes throughout the week, I am overly focused on the next task that must be accomplished while taking little time to truly think about why I am doing certain things or what, if any, satisfaction I derive from it. Volunteering forces me to re-evaluate things, and serves as a reminder to take pause and remember that not everything in life has to be so serious. I feel that my service (i.e., volunteering) is something of value to someone else, which is something that I draw upon after a particularly difficult session with a client. It is in serving others that I derive much joy and satisfaction. It is this joy and satisfaction that keeps me rejuvenated for the challenges ahead.

Boxing—Lindsay Klimik

One of the biggest activities that I do to practice self-care is boxing. I started up about 7 years ago when my college field hockey coach took the team to her boxing gym for a workout. I loved the intensity of the training and the challenge of learning something new, so I picked it up after the season ended. I boxed at a gym for a few years, and tried my hand at sparring in a few matches. After getting hit square in the nose a few times, I decided that fighting wasn't for me. I was more interested in boxing because it was fun and a good workout, not because I wanted to compete.

I had no trouble finding a gym once I moved to a new city for graduate school. I box four to five times a week, whether it is after externship, between classes, or early on the weekend, I make time in my schedule to get a work out in. There is something refreshing about a boxing gym. No frills, no gimmicks, just hard work and a lot of sweat. To box, the essential equipment includes a pair of hand wraps and 12-, 14-, or 16-ounce gloves. It is also helpful to have a jump rope and a bag to hold the gear. Actually learning to box takes time and patience. It is challenging at first to master the foot work, different punches, and speed bag. It is helpful to have a knowledgeable and dedicated trainer to provide feedback and pointers about how to improve. I remember feeling extremely awkward and uncoordinated when I first started, and it took a few months before I felt like I knew what I was doing. The important thing is to stick with it, because the benefits of boxing are worth the frustrations of learning the sport.

I choose to box as my self-care because it is a way to challenge myself, to relieve stress, to stay in shape, and to have fun. When I'm boxing, I don't think about school, or patients, or what I need to do when I get home. I am very much in the moment, focusing on throwing a one, two, or slipping a hook. It is the way that I push my body past what I thought were my limits, and challenge myself mentally not to give up when my muscles are screaming that I should quit. Boxing gives me a feeling of pride in what I have accomplished, and confidence in my abilities. More than the physical and stress-relieving benefits of boxing, the gym has provided me with something I didn't expect, immersion in a culture that I didn't know existed, friendship, and a sense of community. My trainer and friends at the gym have become something of a second family to me. They help hold me accountable, keep me focused and motivated, and challenge me to push myself. I know that no matter how busy, overwhelming, or hectic my life gets, I will always make time to box. It would take more than an exam or dissertation to knock me down, because I'm coming out swinging.

Yoga—Sarah Brager

For the past three years, I have regularly been practicing yoga. I have attended classes mostly at a hot yoga studio in [my local city] but during the past year also in a high-rise building in Bangkok, Thailand, in the fresh air at the base of the Himalayas in Pokhara, Nepal, in a gazebo next to a rice paddy in Bali, Indonesia, as well as in various airports around the world! I've spent as much as 500 Thai baht (around $16.50) for a class and as little as $0. Yoga is my form of self-care. When I am on the mat, my mind is focused on moving through postures and breathing. There is no room to think about the anxieties of grad school or my to-do list when I am in a headstand pose, and if my mind starts to wonder, I know that I will fall flat on my face. Yoga requires you to be completely present and to concentrate fully on the task at hand. I first started practicing yoga by taking a 5-week beginner course at a local yoga studio. I had never participated in a form of exercise that made me feel as good, body and soul, as yoga did. Yoga is my form of self-care because for 90 minutes or however long I choose to practice, my mind is clear and my focus is present.

For somebody who is interested in becoming a yogi or a yogini, I would definitely recommend taking a beginner course to get familiarized with the yoga jargon and the postures. I've seen people of all ages, shapes, and sizes, as well as athletic ability practicing yoga—so don't let any of those things be your excuse! One of the great things about yoga is that it is completely portable. You can attend classes in a studio or on your bedroom floor listening to a podcast. You do not need anything besides your body! On the door of a yoga studio I visited, the following is written, "Ninety minutes of torture, ninety years of healthy life." I would include that the health is not just physical but also mental and spiritual.

Zumba Fitness—Sylvia S. Hanna

My favorite form of self-care is an exercise program called Zumba Fitness. It is a Latin-inspired dance-fitness program that incorporates music and rhythms from around the world into a high-intensity, calorie-burning workout. I stumbled upon my first Zumba Fitness class when a Zumba instructor was asked to sub for another fitness class that I had sporadically been attending at my gym on Saturday mornings. I began taking Zumba once a week and after several weeks, decided I needed more. Over the coming months, I slowly worked up to taking four, five, and even six classes weekly. After six months, I was so "hooked" that I decided to attend a licensing workshop to become a Zumba instructor and eventually began subbing for other instructors in the area.

Most Zumba Fitness classes are about 1 hour long and do not require the participants to have any special equipment. Many gyms offer Zumba classes that are included in the gym membership, and thus, are free to their members. Other classes are held in different locations such as dance studios or recreation centers and those often have an associated fee per class that can range anywhere from about $3 to $10 depending on which area of the country they are offered. The only prerequisite to taking a Zumba class is a desire to have fun! There are no special skills or dance background required. The biggest tip I can offer to a first-time Zumba participant is to simply let go and have fun! Oftentimes people are concerned about their lack of coordination or how they will look, but when you step into a class, you quickly realize that everyone else is focusing on the instructor and is simply there to have a good time while getting a great workout.

Now that I have thoroughly hyped up the Zumba Fitness program, I should backtrack and say that I have always *hated* (yes, *despised*) exercise. But, the more I took Zumba the more I fell in love with the program. The Zumba motto is "Ditch the workout! Join the party!" and indeed, the classes feel like a party! For the first time in my life,

I was truly dedicated to an exercise routine and loved every minute of it! The classes truly are a full-body workout that leaves you drenched in sweat! Zumba was the program that introduced me to all of the mental, emotional, and physical benefits that exercise brings along. Aside from being an incredible stress reliever over the past couple years of graduate school, Zumba has helped me become the healthiest I have ever been and has boosted my confidence. The next time you walk past a Zumba class and hear the music blasting, jump in and experience it for yourself!

Piano Playing —Valerie Faure

I have been playing the piano for 18 years. I was classically trained through private lessons until I was 16, and now I generally play and write my own music. Growing up, I played about 3 to 4 hours per week, though since starting graduate school, I'm lucky if I get 2 hours per week. I started playing the piano when I was 6 years old. My older sister was taking piano lessons and I remember wanting to play, and banging away on the piano (usually when my sister was trying to practice . . .).

Beyond enjoyment, playing the piano taught me discipline, frustration tolerance, perseverance, and how to manage performance anxiety, something I still struggle with today. There were many concerts where, despite having a piece completely memorized and able to play it flawlessly at home, I stumbled and lost my place. I used to get upset when this happened, but I've learned that I notice these flaws more than anybody else, and I try to remember that when, for example, I'm giving a presentation for a class. At this point in my life, "jamming" on the piano is important because it gives me an opportunity to express my creativity, something I don't necessarily get to do a lot of in graduate school. Playing the piano helps me focus; it's nearly impossible to play the piano and multitask. I find that whenever I'm trying to engage in self-care my mind wanders back to worrying about the things I'm *not* doing, or multitasking ([e.g.,] studying while running on a treadmill . . . ineffective AND dangerous!). When I'm playing the piano, I can literally clear my mind and just focus on the music. Similarly, creating music gives me a sense of calm and an opportunity to do something completely "me," and not an assignment for a professor or another report for a client. Another important aspect is convenience: I have a keyboard in my apartment and I can plug in headphones and play anytime, day or night, without bothering anybody.

Lastly, playing the piano helps me connect back to my family. Most members of my extended family grew up playing the piano. I always play at any family function or holiday. My 94-year-old grandma is almost completely deaf so it can be difficult to chat and catch up with her when I see her. But whenever we're together, I'll play for her for hours because she can hear piano music well and loves it. For us, piano music is our common ground. She gets to know the creative me in a way that I don't share with many people.

Faith-Based Choir Group—Arianna Perra

My unique self-care practice is participating in a volunteer choir at my church. I've been involved in my church in a lot of different ways since moving to a new city for graduate school. Pretty quickly I met a lot of kind and interesting people, who over time became an extremely important network of support. Furthermore, having been a musician for much of my life before college and graduate school, I relished the opportunity to make music again.

One of the things that feeds me most about choir is the weekly act of slowing down, shifting gears, and reconnecting with my body as an instrument of how I am in the world. As a clinician, I understand that I am my own best tool, and music is a different way to think about this process. I'm exercising a different part of my brain, which is helpful to give myself a mental break from the day and from the weight of whatever it is that I'm dealing with at the time. I also think that making music every week helps me be a more creative person in general, which increases flexibility in my clinical work as well. Another major piece of singing in the choir as self-care is the role of community. Making music with a group of people requires an awareness and attunement of the people around you, whether it is the pitch and pace of your fellow choristers or cues from the director. Finally, weekly rehearsals are fun and challenging, and no matter how little energy I feel I have when rehearsal starts, the group always picks me up.

I would highly recommend joining a choir to any graduate student with an interest in music. The time commitment is quite small in comparison to what I feel I get out of it; a midweek rehearsal for an hour and a half, 15–20 minutes before service on Sunday and then the hour the service actually takes; essentially, three hours per week. Most of us spend more time than that on Facebook! Many churches have volunteer choirs, which are open to anyone in the community; you do not have to subscribe to that faith in order to sing in the choir (though, if the church stuff gets under your skin, it might not be a great fit). Whether you're looking to join the congregation or the choir, shop around; find a place where you feel comfortable and invited. Don't judge yourself too harshly if you don't think of yourself as a "singer," if you don't read music, or if you haven't sung in umpteen years. In the right choral community, none of that will matter. For me, what does matter is the consistent support of the group, a regular connection to creativity, and a weekly willingness to face that which may be challenging, uncomfortable, or exposing. It's about making a joyful noise.

Animal Rescue/Pet Care—Rachel Lawson

One of my self-care activities involves training and spending time with my rescued dog as well as looking for dogs or cats that need rescuing on the streets. I first rescued my dog Apollo during my second year of graduate school. When I moved to my current city for graduate school I felt a void, and sought an apartment that would allow dogs. I became particularly intrigued with pit bulls because I heard from various individuals that they were commonly abused, fought for monetary gain, and over-running the animal shelters. When I met Apollo I somehow felt it was my personal responsibility to save this dog and any other animals that were mistreated by their owners. Of course, this was an unrealistic goal, however I knew I wanted to be on the lookout for more rescues, at least in order to bring them to a shelter rather than allow them to be neglected or abused in homes like the one from which I rescued Apollo.

Training a dog involves a lot of patience. I used to joke that it was a full-time job on top of full-time schooling to house-train Apollo, teach him basic dog manners, help cure his separation anxiety, and socialize him adequately so he didn't become aggressive. It required patience and flexibility with the quality of my furniture and carpets, and the planning of my schedule, as it basically revolved around him. Financially, I had to pay for the veterinarian bills; I would recommend adopting a dog through a shelter that does basic health screenings before adoption. There is also the additional cost of toys, food, and other dog necessities (crate, leash, etc.). Further, because I live far away from my family, I have to drive rather than fly due to costs and other logistical issues involved with flying long distances with a dog. At times, I also need to pay for people to walk him when I have long days at school or externship.

Dogs are arguably one of the most therapeutic entities on earth! I enjoy the fact that he is always happy to see me and seems to appreciate everything I do for him, even the very little things (like scratching between his ears). Having a dog has also opened the door for meeting many wonderful people. Apollo is often a means for people to initiate friendly conversation with me, either at the pet store, in my travels, or on our daily walks. Particularly in graduate school for psychology when I am tired and exhausted from listening to others about their problems, ailments, and concerns, it is incredibly refreshing and rewarding to have such a rich relationship that does not require such conversation; if that is not self-care, I don't know what is!

Voice of Experience: One Psychologist's Perspective

As I read through these personal descriptions of innovative and creative self-care practices by my graduate students, in addition to being so impressed by their range of talents and interests, I was reminded of a former graduate student who shared with me a video of her tap dancing. She animatedly described to me all the joys of tap dancing, what great fun it is, how much she enjoys the friendships she has made in her tap dance group, and what a great stress reliever it is for her. While my focus on pleasure reading and exercise that includes day hikes on the Appalachian Trail may seem a bit boring in contrast, I find myself inspired by these descriptions of creative self-care strategies and remain open to the possibilities for new activities.

Discover Your Valued Self-Care Activities

Which of the above activities interest you?

Could you picture yourself participating in any of them? If so, please list them below.

List the top five reasons you can think of for *not* participating in them.

List the top five reasons you can think of *for* participating in them.

What are some activities you used to enjoy participating in that you no longer do?

What are some activities you have thought of participating in but never did (regardless of the reasons)?

What qualities or attributes are important to you in practicing self-care? (Check all that apply.)

Creativity   ____
Relaxation   ____
Clearing my mind   ____
Exercising and being active   ____
Socializing/being with others   ____
Quiet time alone   ____
Stimulating my mind   ____
Escaping from my day-to-day activities   ____
Thrill seeking   ____
Learning new skills   ____
Connecting with my personal beliefs/faith   ____
Other qualities that are important to me:

What are some self-care activities that meet the specific needs that you have identified above?

In years to come, when you look back on this time, you will want to feel good about the decisions you made and not feel regret over things you wish you had done. There is no better time than the present to take positive action to start doing the things you really want to do and that will be enjoyable and enriching for you. Write down several activities you might enjoy participating in.

Now make an action plan and implement it!

Part III

From Individual to Community and Beyond

Fostering Networks of Self-Care

Caring for Ourselves and One Another

When a Peer May Have a Problem

Alex, a graduate student in psychology, and her partner of 3 years recently broke up. This separation involved emotional upset for Alex, moving out of the couple's apartment, and the loss of financial assistance from her partner who had at times helped Alex out with day-to-day expenses the couple shared. Since the breakup, Alex's classmates have been noticing that Alex seems "not herself"— including falling behind on several assignments, seeming disorganized and arriving to class late on a few occasions, and appearing to withdraw from other students. Her new roommate, a classmate of Alex's, has noticed her drinking wine each night. Several classmates who work at the same training site as Alex have also noticed her uncharacteristically sounding frustrated and irritated with clients at times, and recently she missed a scheduled appointment with a client. A few peers are beginning to wonder whether they should discuss with Alex the recent changes in her behavior and the impact it is having on her academic and clinical work. They are unsure, however, if this is necessary and, if so, what would be an appropriate way to address her. They worry that she will become more upset and she will think they are gossiping about her or making a "big deal" about nothing. Her peers are also wondering whether they should talk to their program director or inform anyone else of this possible issue, yet they also are concerned about any potential negative impact this may have on Alex's academic career. Some peers have suggested that they keep quiet and mind their own business, leaving the group divided and confused over what to do.

Looking Beyond Ourselves

Much of this book so far has approached self-care and its associated components of psychological wellness as a journey that is unique and individual to you. We have emphasized the importance of staying attuned to your own experiences of personal and professional highs and lows; experiences of stress and its potential associated outcomes; the internal and self-reflective components of monitoring, identifying, and attending to your needs and challenges; your professional competence and ethical behavior; and your overall psychological well-being. Assessing one's own professional well-functioning is typically treated very much as a "private affair."[1]

> *Assessing one's own professional well-functioning is typically treated very much as a "private affair."*

Are we, however, our own best monitors and judges of our competence and overall psychological and emotional wellness? The reality is that it is both "unreasonable and illogical" to expect ourselves to successfully predict, identify, and respond to our own experiences of distress or other potential risk factors.[2] While some may attempt to work through identified issues, far too often many of us are either not aware of or choose to ignore the effects of the challenges we face.[3]

Take a moment to consider how at one time or another, you have experienced receiving honest feedback, whether solicited or not, from family or friends about items of your clothing. Often this feedback suggests that you may have missed the mark or failed to see what others see: as if when you had looked in the mirror that morning to put on those clothes you had seen something different than everyone else. Whether a polite "Maybe it is time to donate that sweater?" or more explicit "What were you thinking?!" the comment opens your eyes to consider something you may not have noticed about yourself. Although this is a rather trivial example, what if we expanded it further: What would the implications be if you could not evaluate your clinical and professional competence, your ethical behavior, and your psychological well-being?

A Skewed Perspective

It would be great, and far easier, if we could always fairly and accurately view and self-evaluate all areas of our lives. But the truth is, we cannot. While we continually stress self-assessment and monitoring in regard to our psychological well-being, the inherent challenge is that we all have blind spots. The professional blind spots we are all at risk for experiencing throughout our careers can make it difficult to engage in accurate self-assessment.[4] Additionally, we are particularly at risk for inaccurately assessing ourselves in areas in which we have deficits.[5] Thus, when experiencing problems with professional competence or other deficits in professional or personal functioning, we are less likely to see the situation clearly.

- A study of college students' expectations and actual performance on an exam revealed that those who performed in the bottom 25% percentile on the exam were the most likely to overestimate their performance by approximately 30%.[6]
- When medical residents were asked to self-assess their interviewing skills with patients, they demonstrated difficulty in providing accurate self-assessment, and those in the lowest performing group were most likely to provide inaccurate and inflated self-assessments.[7]

Where might your blind spots be when evaluating yourself? As an emerging professional responsible for maintaining ethical and competent practice, what can you expect to do and rely on to address this inherent challenge when it comes to self-monitoring and self-assessment of your professional competence and psychological well-being?

Despite the inherently skewed perspectives each of us has, all is not lost. Since your own individual assessment of your competence and overall personal and professional well-being is not 100% reliable and can result in potentially significant and harmful risks, it is important for you, and all of us, to look to our colleagues and peers to assist us—to provide us with that realistic view we may not be able to see for ourselves. In turn, we must provide such assistance and monitoring for our peers and colleagues; we must all look out for each other. The importance of monitoring the competence, functioning, and well-being of your peers and colleagues and of them in turn monitoring you is vital in fostering a "culture of prevention" and safe practice.[8]

Voice of Experience: One Psychologist's Perspective

I can definitely report that I carefully pay attention to my level of stress, feelings of fatigue, and signs of burnout. Yet, several years ago I changed my work balance to see fewer clients in my practice and spend more time teaching, writing, mentoring students, and so forth. I was amazed to observe that when I shifted my private practice from full time to part time, the number and percentage of clients who terminated treatment prematurely and the number of "no-shows" went down dramatically. While I wasn't aware of any difficulties while seeing clients full time, and I know I was a competent psychologist who helped lots of clients, there clearly was something going on that was impacting my effectiveness with clients. Despite all my best efforts and sensitivity to these issues, my own self-assessment and self-awareness of difficulties was quite limited. It wasn't that I didn't care or wasn't interested in this; I just didn't have the ability to see and experience myself as others did. In retrospect, I can see how important it is to have colleagues who can assist me with my awareness of my functioning and assessment of my competence, and the need to actively use these colleagues in this way.

The Challenge for Graduate Students

Not only is relying solely on your own self-assessment of your competence unreliable and risky at any stage of your professional career, as a graduate student the tasks of assessing, identifying, and responding to your risk factors and challenges to competence can be particularly difficult. Unlike the seasoned professional you will one day be, at this early stage of your professional career, it may be difficult to rely on experience and perspective that can be helpful in identifying when you are experiencing distress, burnout, and problems with professional competence. There is little opportunity to put things in perspective ("I remember the last time I was having this challenge, or feeling this way . . .") and using this perspective as a guide. Additionally, without this perspective, it may be more challenging for you to identify signs or symptoms in the earlier stages, while they are developing and before they become more pronounced.

Lacking familiarity or previous experience with these issues, it can sometimes be challenging to, for example, tease apart gradations of signs of stress compared to more significant signs of distress or burnout. Furthermore, fear of evaluation may inhibit or discourage you from reaching out to faculty or supervisors for support upon identifying problems, given the nature of these relationships.[9] Some faculty and supervisors who have had limited training in addressing graduate students with professional competence problems may find such conversations with trainees to be challenging and difficult. At times this may, unfortunately, contribute to the avoidance of such necessary conversations.[10]

Having your competence constantly monitored as a graduate student, you may also feel a pull to actively try to conceal signs or evidence that you are experiencing challenges or difficulties. Be aware that feelings of shame or competitiveness, or perhaps having unrealistic expectations of yourself, may extend beyond inhibiting disclosure of issues to faculty and prompt you to not share your difficulties with peers, friends, and family as well.

As mentioned previously in this book, many graduate programs fail to recognize when students are at risk or struggling, fail to have fortified intervention plans in place for students who may be exhibiting signs of problems with professional competence, and lack clear identified roles and responsibilities among evaluators.[11] Even when graduate programs do identify and address students experiencing competence issues, because of the inherent nature of such evaluation processes, problems must be identified before any form of intervention takes place. This approach works against the promotion of prevention and identifying potential issues before they become significant and damaging for you and those you treat. Such evaluation processes are also often conducted in a concealed and confidential manner.[12] As a result, you may feel uncertain about whether faculty are aware of and addressing the issues a peer is experiencing, and uncertain about how to respond to such an identified peer.[13]

Faculty members and graduate students alike must work to stamp out this "culture of silence" surrounding student professional competence issues that has been maintained in many academic and training institutions.[14] This lack of proper attention in identifying and attending to competence issues may likely perpetuate the isolating nature of this process, thereby further complicating your ability and opportunity to accurately view and assess your own competence as a trainee.

Competence Constellations

We each are vulnerable to the effects of stress and the risk of developing problems of professional competence as we are confronted with different challenges at each stage of development throughout our careers. Assess for risk factors and signs of problems with professional competence in both yourself and your peers. Such assessments should not be one-time events, but conducted as part of an ongoing process. While passing the Examination for Professional Practice of Psychology (EPPP) and gaining licensure are surely milestone accomplishments, they are neither the final stage nor the sole standard in your assessment and demonstration of competence.

As the foundation of your professional development is being laid during your time in graduate school, it is important to understand and practice "communitarian ethics." [15] We cannot stand alone and rely solely on our own means and abilities to accurately and ethically recognize and respond to times of challenge, distress, and risks to competence. Rather, we must build and engage in "competence constellations"—networks comprised of peers and colleagues, consultation groups, supervisors, and professional associations—for continual competence assessment. [16] We must develop and participate in competence constellations to protect and promote our own competence as well as to benefit our fellow peers and colleagues.

How do you create a competence constellation? Identify a network of support around you, a diverse network of individuals representing various aspects of your personal and professional life who have access to monitoring your professional competence and well-being.[17] This network is made up of several tiers, representing the various degrees of closeness and connection you have with those who are part of your competence constellation. Below you will

We must develop and participate in competence constellations to protect and promote our own competence as well as to benefit our fellow peers and colleagues.

find suggestions for types of individuals who may make up your competence constellation. Practicing communitarian ethics by creating your own competence constellation and monitoring the well-functioning of peers and colleagues may contribute to decreased frequency and severity of problems with professional competence. It may also foster greater openness and diminished feelings of shame regarding imperfections, emotional distress, and any needs for assistance with colleagues.[18]

Building Your Competence Constellation

Inner Core—Tier 1
- Close professional friends
- Career mentor
- Personal psychotherapist
- Spouse/partner

Collegial Community—Tier 2
- Coworkers
- Supervisor
- Consultant
- Consultation group members
- Colleagues from professional or community organizations

Collegial Acquaintances—Tier 3
- Professional acquaintances/formal professional friends

Professional Culture—Tier 4
- All who contribute to the culture of the profession (e.g., the ethical principles, norms, and standards of profession)[19]

These tiers of your competence constellation are not static and unmoving.[20] They are flexible and dynamic as members of the constellation may move up and down the tiers over time as relationships change. For example, a collegial acquaintance with whom you begin working on a project can easily move into Tier 2, becoming a part of your collegial community as you spend more time interacting with each other. In fact, over time, as you get to know each other better and support each other more, this colleague can move into Tier 1, becoming someone on whom you increasingly rely for support and friendship. Similarly, you and an individual who had previously been close friends may grow apart over time, spending less time together, moving him or her into Tier 2, where he or she remains a part of your collegial community but just not as important a part of it as in the past when in Tier 1.

Easier Said than Done?

Despite the ethical responsibility, intervening with a peer or colleague exhibiting professional competence problems can be a challenging task.

- Psychotherapists who have addressed a colleague exhibiting signs of professional competence problems typically have more years of licensed experience than those who have not had experience addressing a colleague.[21]
- Commonly noted problems experienced by graduate students as reported by peers have included
  - professional behavior problems,
  - clinical concerns,
  - academic skill problems,
  - psychological difficulties (e.g., mood disorders, personality disorders or traits, anxiety disorders, eating disorders, substance abuse problems),
  - burnout,
  - lack of timely preparedness, and
  - interpersonal concerns.[22]
- Among 44% of graduate student respondents who reported having experience with a fellow trainee's professional competence problems, less than 60% took some action

regarding the peer, although this typically did not involve directly addressing the peer.[23]

- Other studies indicate that approximately 85–95% of graduate students surveyed report having worked with or been aware of at least one problematic peer during their graduate school experience, yet only 33–42% of them addressed the peer directly.[24]

Challenges to Intervening

Why might graduate students and psychotherapists resist intervening when it is indicated? One reason is that while some signs of professional competence problems may be more readily apparent to peers or colleagues (e.g., peer dynamics, quality of work, substance abuse symptoms) some signs of distress, burnout, and secondary traumatic stress may be easier for peers or colleagues to overlook due to the "personal nature" of such symptoms.[25] Additional challenges to be mindful of include the following:

- Beliefs that the peer's problems do not impact his or her work performance
- Lack of evidence regarding the peer's deteriorated professional functioning
- Uncertainty about one's professional responsibility to intervene
- Expectation of a negative outcome
- Perceived risk to yourself or your peer[26]

Given the dynamics of graduate school and peer relations, you may also be at risk of feeling resentful and confused regarding a peer with professional competence problems, and may not know how to respond or what actions to take.[27] It is common to feel resentment toward the peer experiencing difficulty, because fellow students may be asked take on additional work to carry the load, and potentially toward faculty if fellow students perceive that the issue is being ignored or not being attended to properly or effectively.[28] You may also consider it not your responsibility to address a peer exhibiting professional competence issues, assuming that faculty or training directors have recognized and are aware of the difficulties the peer has been demonstrating. Take some time to consider what may serve as a roadblock for you to intervene with a peer or colleague when intervention is called for.

Have you worried about a peer or felt that the peer exhibited signs of problems of professional competence? To what extent did you feel faculty members and administrators in your graduate program were aware of this? Interestingly, graduate students are typically more confident that faculty or supervisors are aware of trainees experiencing professional competence problems and less confident that these faculty or supervisors would actually address the problematic trainee.[29] Keep in mind that given the size, nature, and dynamics of many graduate programs, you as the student may be more likely to notice or be aware of fellow students' difficulties than faculty, or may recognize the signs of problems earlier or before they become more significant and noticeable to faculty. Therefore, relying solely on faculty to notice and take action regarding a student who may be demonstrating signs of professional competence problems may be a misguided approach that may result in the student's problems and needs being overlooked, ignored, or not adequately addressed.

When Prevention Is Not Enough: When and How to Intervene

Sometimes action beyond prevention is necessary. Knowing when and how to intervene with a peer can appear daunting and inhibit you from taking action. Yet choosing to ignore or defer to others the responsibility of monitoring and addressing a peer or colleague experiencing professional competence issues contributes only to "perpetuating dysfunctional patterns."[30] While there is no one-size-fits-all model or instruction manual when it comes to intervening, the following suggestions may help guide you through the process and help make it a positive experience for both you and your peer(s).

First, keep in mind that prevention is always the gold standard when it comes to self-care and psychological wellness. Therefore, if unsure whether a peer or colleague is exhibiting early signs of distress (and thus questioning whether intervention is necessary) or more advanced signs of burnout and professional competence issues, do not wait for more clear evidence or more significant symptoms before raising these issues or expressing your concerns with the peer. The longer you wait, the greater potential risk of harm to both your colleague and his or her clients. Speak with this peer to prevent these issues from escalating to more serious symptoms of burnout or professional competence problems.

Talking with a Peer

- Consider location and timing. Invite the person to grab lunch or coffee so that you can talk more privately and leisurely.
- Consult with a faculty member, supervisor, and/or another peer for guidance in this discussion when appropriate.
- Express concern and empathy, and avoid accusatory tones.
- Take time to consider resources to suggest prior to the conversation.
- Remember that you do not need all the details about the person if he or she is experiencing issues. Rather, your goal is to inform the person of your concern and encourage positive change.

Taking your peer aside and empathically noting your concerns and observations may be all that is needed to make the person aware of the issue. Take a "supportive and non-antagonistic approach" in expressing your concern.[31] For a peer who may be feeling isolated, alone, overwhelmed, or other similar and challenging feelings, reaching out to the person in this way may prove to be the first step in the peer seeking and receiving needed help, support, and assistance. If the peer is already aware and wants to discuss with you his or her recognition of it, together you can share ideas regarding how to address the issue(s). Or, if the peer expresses recognition and has made efforts toward remediation, you can continue to be supportive as he or she goes through this process.

If informal and direct communication with the peer or colleague does not result in his or her actions or steps toward beginning to attend to these problems of professional competence, the next ethical step is then contacting, informing, and seeking action from people in the appropriate groups, such as your graduate or training department or, later on in your career, licensing and regulatory boards or professional organizations. Such steps are clearly an ethical responsibility.

But it should be emphasized that the formal reporting of unethical behavior is a last resort. The preventive actions described earlier, which are based on concern and caring for our peers and colleagues, are recommended as our initial response when concerns arise.

You may also benefit from asking about the resources within your graduate or training program. Learning about how graduate students are evaluated for competence and how the program responds when issues are identified (e.g., meetings, review boards) can be helpful. It may also be informative and useful for future reference to inquire about temporary leaves of absence, mandated or voluntary individual psychotherapy, or temporary reduced workload accommodations. Become familiar with such resources and processes early on as a preventive strategy, rather than waiting to experience problems or issues to learn about them.

Programs run by professional organizations can also be helpful. Ask whether any colleague assistance or support-related programs are offered by professional organizations you belong to. Finally, personal psychotherapy (see Chapter 8) can be a particularly important self-care tool for graduate students or colleagues experiencing professional competence problems.

Support Down the Road . . .

A number of additional resources are available for psychologists in the area of colleague assistance. While these services provide limited support or programs for graduate students, it is important to become familiar with these resources in case they are needed in the future by either you or a colleague struggling with professional competence issues.

- For APA members, colleague assistance programs, generally established through state, provincial, and territorial psychological associations (SPTPAs) and overseen by the APA's Advisory Committee on Colleague Assistance (ACCA), aim to address the needs of psychologists who are currently experiencing problems with professional competence.[32]
- Services offered by colleague assistance programs include consultation and referrals for psychologists experiencing distress, burnout, and problems with professional competence.[33]

Whether a first-year graduate student or a seasoned professional, the profession of psychology demands continued assessment and monitoring of your professional competence and psychological well-being to ensure safe, ethical, and competent clinical practice. Often, your efforts to self-assess your competence and respond with appropriate self-care practices are individual and isolated experiences. But this should not be the sole means for ensuring proper and accurate identification, monitoring, and response when you are experiencing signs and symptoms of distress and professional competence issues. Looking beyond your own vistas and engaging with peers and colleagues in a community of monitoring and looking out for one another, starting today as a graduate student, is a critical practice for fostering a focus on prevention. We must each be our professional brothers' and sisters' keepers of competence and well-being.

Responding to Alex

Alex's peers should approach and speak to her in a supportive and nonconfrontational manner. They should begin by inquiring about how she is doing personally and professionally, asking whether she has noticed any changes or challenges for herself, and expressing their concerns. They should find out about steps she may have already taken to address the issue, and encourage her to seek additional support by talking with faculty and considering personal psychotherapy (if not doing so already), and recommend that she continue reaching out to peers. It also is important for her peers to check in with Alex over time and provide continued encouragement and support, as one's responsibility to another peer or colleague is not limited to a one-time event or obligation that can then be forgotten or done with. Other options for Alex's peers include consulting with their program director, training director, or supervisor. It may also be helpful to establish a peer support group: both for Alex's classmates, to discuss their difficulties in navigating this situation, and for Alex.

Key Points to Remember About Peer and Colleague Assistance
- Our abilities to accurately assess our own competence, particularly during times of distress, are limited.
- While our self-care journey is often individualized and unique, monitoring our psychological wellness and professional competence cannot be entirely internal and isolated.

- We have a responsibility to ensure accurate assessment of the competence of ourselves and our peers, and for the continual practice of safe and best practices for our clients by engaging in communitarian ethics and continuously monitoring the competence of our colleagues.
- Prevention is key. Monitoring and addressing peers at the early stages of signs or symptoms can reduce more significant and graver implications for peers and their clients later on.
- Remember that the values and habits you develop now as a graduate student will significantly influence your professional identity down the road. How you choose to approach and take part in monitoring and tending to the self-care needs of peers and colleagues, as well as your own, will lay the foundation for how you will approach and handle such situations in the future.

Building "Competence Constellations"

Consider the idea of "competence constellations."[34] Who in your professional community and personal life would you consider part of your constellation? Complete the activity below, considering all four tiers of the competence constellation network,[35] identifying individuals, groups, and/or organizations you can currently rely on to be part of your constellation and that take part in monitoring your competence and well-being.

My Competence Constellation

INNER CORE—TIER 1

-

-

-

COLLEGIAL COMMUNITY—TIER 2

-

-

-

COLLEGIAL ACQUAINTANCES—TIER 3

-

-

-

PROFESSIONAL CULTURE—TIER 4

-

-

-

Building My Competence Constellation: Future Additions

Are there people, resources, or groups that you can add to this constellation to build its supportive network further? Are there some individuals who are not presently a part of your competence constellation who might be good additions? Are there individuals at one tier who you might like to be a greater part of your competence constellation? How would you go about making these changes?

Now, consider what competence constellations you may be part of for others, holding the responsibility of monitoring and tending to the competent care and practice of others.

•

•

•

•

•

How can you more actively utilize and participate in your competence constellations? What actions should you take to more actively participate in them? List three things you can begin doing now.

1.

2.

3.

Reflection Activity

Because prevention is always the primary goal, what actions can you take to develop and actively utilize your competence constellations prior to experiencing problems with professional competence? Having these in place and utilizing them actively may serve a key role in addressing any difficulties you may experience early on in the development of these difficulties, and thus preventing or reducing serious consequences to self or others.

Creating a Culture of Self-Care in Your Graduate Program

Self-Care in the Graduate School Program: Mission Impossible?

Derron is a graduate student in a small, competitive graduate program. He finds himself frustrated when professors throw around comments such as "And remember self-care!" but do not explain it, or discuss how to actually do it, particularly when they are also assigning many tasks, are aware of midterms approaching, and know that Derron and his peers have been very busy adjusting to their training site and to graduate school in general. After reading a book about self-care, Derron has begun to incorporate some self-care practices into his daily routine, but given the culture of his program—receiving e-mails from professors at 3 a.m., peers discussing who slept the fewest hours, and remembering one professor's comment on the first day of school that students were expected to show dedication to their program and training by essentially putting their lives on hold until graduation—he feels that this will be difficult to maintain. Derron feels stuck in an unhealthy academic environment and wonders whether there is any way he can change things for himself, his cohort, and even his program without overstepping bounds or hitting a brick wall.

The Graduate School Environment

As you assess your personal and professional challenges and sources of distress, gain awareness and insight into your risks for burnout and problems with professional competence, and begin your unique and personal journey of self-care, you will see how these largely individual challenges and self-care practices are often wedded within and tied to the larger environmental contexts of graduate school. Self-care not only is a vital element of your professional identity at the micro level, focusing on individual needs and lifestyles, but must also be addressed at the macro level, attending to the overall graduate school and training environments that you are part of. While your individual self-care efforts are extremely important, it is vital to keep in mind that you are functioning within a larger system that can place numerous, often competing, demands on you.

While your individual self-care efforts are extremely important, it is vital to keep in mind that you are functioning within a larger system that can place numerous, often competing, demands on you.

Every faculty member may believe that every one of the readings he or she assigns is important and essential to your education. Similarly, clinical supervisors may assign additional readings, recordings to review, and other activities to promote your "essential" professional development. Your research supervisor may want extensive revisions of your literature review completed over the weekend and turned in first thing Monday morning. The fact that each of these individuals is placing demands on your time without coordinating assignments with the others can place you under great pressure and even create impossible situations. And none of this takes into consideration the realities of your personal life, or even the fact that you have (or are trying to have) one.

Practicing self-care without consideration of the ongoing demands of, and challenges within, your professional environment and without its adequate support may prove to be both frustrating and ineffective. If your professional environment and the communities within these environments—which may include involvement in areas of academics, clinical placements, research, and the like—have unrealistic expectations, do not coordinate demands and expectations, and do not provide adequate support in your efforts at self-care, you may begin to feel like Sisyphus, forever pushing a boulder up a hill but never reaching the top.

The Current Status of Self-Care Education in Graduate Programs

"We need to improve the psychological healthiness of our training programs."[1] It is important to examine the extent to which many graduate programs are attending to the education and promotion of self-care. Each graduate program has its own unique culture. Take time to reflect specifically on the environment of your graduate program in regard to self-care (see evaluation exercise at the end of this chapter). As a whole, however, the promotion of self-care, and focus on the importance and use of self-care for prevention of increased distress, burnout, and problems with professional competence, appears to be limited or absent from many graduate programs.

The following information, obtained by a survey conducted by APA's ACCA, sheds light on the absence of self-care promotion in graduate programs:

"We need to improve the psychological healthiness of our training programs."

- 82.8% of graduate student respondents reported that their training program did not offer written materials on self-care and stress,
- 63.4% reported that their program did not sponsor activities promoting self-care,
- 59.3% reported that their training program did not informally promote a self-care atmosphere,
- 31% of graduate students reported that psychotherapy was encouraged but not required in their program, and
- only 9% stated that psychotherapy was required for all students in training.[2]

A review of the *Guidelines and Principles for Accreditation of Programs in Professional Psychology* created by the APA's Commission on Accreditation indicates no mention of the promotion or practice of self-care or well-being of students under the guiding principles or accreditation standards for doctoral graduate programs.[3] Additionally, many faculty members and supervisors within graduate programs do not provide adequate models of self-care for their students to follow.[4] This can include faculty members or supervisors continuing to work when too distressed to be effective, not practicing a self-care regimen, or not giving enough attention to their personal life and failing to balance the personal with the professional realm.

What Graduate Programs Can Do

The graduate school environment presents many challenges to implementing a lifestyle of self-care for graduate students. Throughout this book, it is likely that you have found yourself at one point or another acknowledging the importance of incorporating self-care into your life and beginning to develop a self-care plan, yet recognizing areas in which these efforts may be challenged or thwarted given the barriers to self-care presented by your graduate program or training site. Receiving e-mails from professors at all hours of the day and night, modeling the expectation that you will also work throughout the night, or scheduling required lectures or events during evening or weekend hours are just some representative examples. What are some of the examples you have faced in graduate school that seem to thwart self-care lifestyles?

Despite the challenges of the nature of graduate school, along with programs that limit support or even discourage self-care, all is not lost. Many recommendations in the literature call attention to the ways in which graduate programs, faculty, supervisors, and administrators can improve procedures to address distress, problems with professional competence, and burnout, and to improve self-care among their graduate students. The following is a list of recommendations that graduate programs may implement to create a "culture of wellness and prevention":[5]

- Provide training seminars to educate students on self-care practices and the risk factors for problems with professional competence.
- Create self-care activities within the program.
- Discuss distress and problems with professional competence during practicum meetings and supervision.
- Consider requiring or strongly encouraging personal psychotherapy.

- Offer affordable opportunities for students to receive psychotherapy.
- Establish student support groups that discuss distress and problems with professional competence.[6]

Voice of Experience: One Psychologist's Perspective

At the school where I teach, I meet with the first-year doctoral students as a group in the first week of their first semester to discuss self-care, wellness promotion, balance, and burnout prevention. I share with them the realities of graduate school, challenges with balance they will experience, and pressures that are likely. We review proactive strategies to utilize as well as ways they can work collaboratively and support one another as a group. I then check in with them periodically to see how they are doing. Our department hosts many self-care activities, including a pleasure reading book co-op that is situated right across from the students' mailboxes in our department. We also host social events each semester such as the "PsyD Olympics," faculty–student softball games (the faculty have yet to even come close to winning!), and outings such as student picnics, happy hours, and major league baseball games. We have student representatives on our doctoral and master's committees, and they regularly provide the faculty with feedback on the environment in our programs.

What Can You Do? The Graduate Student Role

In addition to the recommendation that graduate programs recognize and adapt to improve the psychological wellness of their programmatic environments, it is also important to recognize your role and the ways in which you too can work to promote healthy environments that encourage positive self-care lifestyles within your training program.

Communication and Atmosphere

One significant way to help create a culture of self-care in your graduate program is to encourage and practice open and active

One significant way to help create a culture of self-care in your graduate program is to encourage and practice open and active communication. communication. Take responsibility for promoting a culture or atmosphere of self-care and wellness in your department and program. Do you and your peers communicate in ways that foster support and encouragement or competition? Can you openly admit to peers, faculty, or supervisors when you feel overwhelmed and anticipate supportive reactions from them, or do you often hold back from acknowledging particularly stressful times in fear of appearing weak or receiving negative feedback and evaluations? Do students and faculty more often praise the student who looks overworked and fatigued for devoting countless hours to work and appearing as the overachiever while labeling another student as an underachiever, or not as serious enough a graduate student, for arriving to class refreshed and having slept 8 hours the night before?

You can play a powerful role in shaping the culture of your cohort and overall program. Engage in open communication with peers that acknowledges times of challenge and distress, that extends support and encouragement to fellow peers, and that sends messages of valuing and promoting lifestyles of balance and self-care. This can have a significant influence on promoting and advocating for a positive and healthy program environment.

Asking for and Promoting Self-Care in Your Program

If your graduate program or training site does not promote self-care or provide self-care education, consider discussing this with administrators and making specific requests for inclusion of these learning opportunities in the program curricula. For example, many graduate programs offer training seminars or invite speakers for one-time events on topics that may not be covered in the traditional course syllabi. Some graduate programs may be open to suggestions from their students on topics or speakers related to self-care. Presentations may include information about the realities of the profession, such as the demanding and challenging work that is involved, and self-care as a normative and necessary lifelong component of being a mental health professional.[7]

Some graduate programs also require students to complete feedback forms at the end of the semester or host meetings at which students can discuss with administrators areas of improvement for the graduate program. Programs that have class or cohort representatives who meet with program administrators periodically can also serve as a great resource for sharing student needs and expectations in the areas of self-care and wellness promotion. Inquire about these types of opportunities, and actively utilize them to promote active change within your program's environment and culture.

Create Peer-Support Groups

Peer support, considered a positive, career-sustaining self-care practice, has been found among surveyed psychotherapists to be the most important contributing factor to their well-functioning.[8] You can create peer-support groups within your own graduate program that can serve as an important self-care practice for you individually as well as have significant influence in fostering a culture of self-care within the overall environment of your graduate program. Beyond peer-support groups, the use of listservs and involvement in professional organizations are other examples of peer support, and are among the seven most frequently used coping strategies endorsed by surveyed psychologists.[9]

> *Peer support, considered a positive, career-sustaining self-care practice, has been found among surveyed psychotherapists to be the most important contributing factor to their well-functioning.*

How is peer support different from group supervision with peers, you may ask? Peer-support groups can provide you with a needed outlet and valuable support to address issues regarding professional challenges or personal problems.[10] The primary goals and intentions of group supervision are focused on monitoring your clinical work, furthering understanding of yourself as a clinician, and of your clients in the context of interacting with and sharing feedback with supervisors and fellow supervisees.[11] Peer support, on the other hand, may provide an opportunity to discuss some clinical issues; however, it is not intended or designed to meet the needs and goals of clinical supervision. Rather, content of peer-support groups typically involves discussion of problematic cases, sources of stress, personal conflicts, and ethical matters.[12] Furthermore, this is done within the context of members providing support for one another in a safe and non-evaluative environment. Trust and confidentiality are key factors in creating a successful peer-support group, in that these factors enable group members to "receive support of fellow travelers" in peer-support groups.[13]

The group format of peer-support allows for the normalization of issues being discussed, encourages the feelings that distress is experienced by all, and that you should not feel ashamed of or retreat from your feelings of distress.[14] Hearing other graduate students relate similar stories of challenges in their clinical work, research, and internship searches, the impact of graduate school on their personal lives, financial stressors related to graduate school, and so forth, can help you recognize that you are not alone in experiencing the stresses of this professional journey. If you work at a training site without many fellow trainees or colleagues to interact with on a daily basis beyond weekly supervision meetings, establishing or becoming a member of a peer-support group can be especially important for addressing professional isolation.[15]

You can work to create and promote peer-support groups within your graduate program and training sites. Peer-support groups can be designed to meet weekly or monthly, designating time to meet during a lunch hour, in the evenings or weekends, or during an open block of time between classes. Having a small number of dedicated members (4 to 10), a private meeting place, and an established regular meeting time are also important logistical elements when establishing a peer-support group.[16]

Consider expanding your peer-support group beyond classmates within your cohort, program, or training site. Often, including a variety of graduate students from multiple schools or training sites and different levels of training can provide unique and diverse perspectives and experiences. Students presenting with new or challenging experiences may hear from other students who have already been through related experiences. This exchange of information provides a degree of normalization, enables learning about what did and did not work for these students, and provides guidance and support from those who have already experienced these situations. The ultimate goal of the program is to establish a group of peers who feel safe, open, and supported to share their thoughts, feelings, and experiences.

Real-Life Reflections on Creating a Peer-Support Group

My classmates and I (LC) created a peer-support group for our class during the second year of our graduate program. This was during a time when many of us were experiencing some challenges in orienting ourselves to clinical work as well as ongoing obstacles of working on our dissertations, balancing life and graduate school, and so on. Although we did not meet often, during the times we did meet, I found it helpful to share my experiences and hear from classmates about their experiences, as I had previously felt as though I was the only one dealing with some of these issues. It was nice to take the time for myself, reflect, and receive support from peers in this way.

A colleague reports a similar experience: "I remember a few of us trying very hard to make this group ongoing and to find dedicated members to commit. Unfortunately, I think there was a huge bystander effect among classmates. I imagine it would have been more helpful if it was encouraged by our graduate program and began as soon as we started doing clinical work."[17]

Professional Organizations

As previously mentioned, state, provincial, and territorial psychological associations (SPTPAs; see Chapter 11), various divisions of the APA, and other professional associations may offer support-type programs and resources for graduate students. Each APA division focuses on a particular area of interest within the field of psychology, and there is at least one division for everyone. Also, most have graduate student sections and membership at significantly reduced rates for students. Here are some examples that may be of relevance and interest for many graduate students:

- Society of Clinical Psychology (Division 12)
- Society of Counseling Psychology (Division 17)
- Division of Psychotherapy (Division 29)
- Psychologists in Independent Practice (Division 42)
- Society for Lesbian, Gay, Bisexual, and Transgender Concerns (Division 44)

Each of these APA divisions has a student section that offers a range of opportunities and resources for student members. For a full list of APA divisions and the resources and opportunities available for graduate students go to http://www.apa.org/about/division/activities/for-students.aspx.

You may also consider becoming an active member of the American Psychological Association for Graduate Students (APAGS) or local professional organizations in your area that may offer an array of programs and benefits that can serve as positive self-care measures for graduate students and offer peer-support outlets. Graduate student members of these groups may have access to listservs, blogs or forums, invitations to events targeted to graduate students, mentoring programs, opportunities to connect with other graduate students outside of your program, and more. As many of these organizations are statewide or national, they can enable you to interact with students from other programs and provide a forum to share concerns and ideas related to the self-care environments of your graduate programs. Active members can also become involved in planning events associated with these organizations at their own graduate programs in order to promote a culture of self-care and encourage increased peer participation in these organizations. Find out whether your graduate program offers financial aid awards or professional development funds to assist graduate students in paying membership dues. If these do not exist, work with your graduate program to help establish such a resource.

Promoting a Self-Care Culture in Your Cohort

Not only does each graduate program have its own unique culture, but each cohort within a single graduate program usually has specific dynamics and characteristics unique to this group of individuals. Consider the culture of your own cohort. In what ways does your cohort promote self-care and psychological wellness? In what ways does it discourage them? Furthermore, given the dynamics and characteristics of your particular cohort, what positive self-care practices or activities would suit your cohort? There are many ways a cohort can come together. For example, you can create an e-mail listserv among your cohort. This can be a helpful way to easily communicate, throw out a question to your classmates, seek feedback, or look for support or guidance from your classmates. Just as ideas for your own self-care practices are limitless, there are countless creative and unique ways to foster a self-care culture within your cohort. Here are some additional ideas:

- Organize a monthly potluck or other social event to promote balance and socialization outside of the graduate program.
- Join an intramural sports team with members of your cohort.
- Create a birthday club to celebrate peers' birthdays.
- Organize study groups, or invite a fellow classmate to do work with you at a local coffee shop.
- Take a walk with several peers during lunchtime.
- Encourage group social events outside of school that promote inclusion of family members, significant others, and friends.
- Inform faculty, supervisors, and administrators of these activities to help promote attendance and emphasize the importance of self-care within the cohort.

One Student's Experience

On the very first day of graduate school, my (LC) cohort created an e-mail listserv for our class. It was intended to ask questions about upcoming assignments, send out the occasional interesting article related to psychology, or to invite classmates to social events. While we have certainly used the listserv for these reasons, over the years we have also used it to reach out to classmates for support after a stressful day, recounting difficult clinical experiences, sharing frustrations, offering humorous stories, and overall providing a culture of openness and honesty about the highs and lows of our graduate school experience. It is a daily self-care practice used and enjoyed by my cohort.

Your personal self-care practices play a significant role in helping you to maintain balance and reduce the risk of problems with professional competence. Remember, however, that you are also part of the complex and multifaceted system of your graduate program. Although some graduate programs continuously work to ensure the education, modeling, and encouragement of self-care lifestyles among their graduate students, more often than not graduate programs are struggling to provide such environments. While those responsible for graduate programs and training sites bear some responsibility, it is important as a graduate student to recognize and actively attend to your role as well in fostering a culture of self-care. The graduate school experience can feel isolating, challenging, nebulous, and overwhelming at times. Creating an environment that encourages positive self-care, where you and your fellow graduate students feel supported and able to share the highs and lows of this experience, can not only provide an invaluable experience during graduate school, but also can set the stage for continued creation and use of a self-care culture with colleagues throughout your career.

Evaluating Your Graduate Program Self-Care Culture

Complete the following informal measure to assess the self-care culture of your graduate program and the degree to which a healthy environment and positive self-care culture is promoted. Consider the degree to which each descriptive is characteristic of your program at present.

	Not at All		Some		Very Much
Competition among peers	0	1	2	3	4
Faculty modeling of positive self-care	0	1	2	3	4
Overall program's openness to graduate student feedback	0	1	2	3	4
Opportunities/outlets to discuss challenges, feelings, and reactions in supportive/non-evaluative ways (e.g., peer-support groups)	0	1	2	3	4
Open communication and support among peers when applying to similar training sites, internship process, research positions, and so forth	0	1	2	3	4
Self-care education incorporated into curricula and training (materials, lectures, speakers, etc.)	0	1	2	3	4
Cliques/interpersonal difficulties among cohort	0	1	2	3	4
Formal procedures regularly used in program to receive graduate student feedback	0	1	2	3	4
Support and encouragement for success and achievements of peers	0	1	2	3	4

Reflection Activity

What role do you currently play within your graduate program's self-care culture? To what extent do you do things that promote competition or maladaptive self-care practices? To what extent do you do things that promote a supportive environment and positive self-care practices within your program?

What changes do you think would be helpful in your program? What role can you play in promoting these changes? What can you and your classmates do together to promote these changes? Consider and reflect on members of faculty and/or administration with whom you can speak about promoting a culture of self-care within your graduate program. What can you ask them to do that may help promote this culture?

Identify three ways in which you believe you can contribute to enhancing the promotion of a positive self-care culture within your graduate program.

1.

2.

3.

Conclusion

To truly understand and help your clients and those you treat, you must first come to know, understand, and care for yourself. Consider the instruction that flight attendants provide each time you fly on an airplane: In case of an emergency, you are to place your own oxygen mask on first, before helping those next to you.[1] While this may sound like a challenging and selfish instruction, it is rooted in the notion that you cannot help those around you if you have not made sure to take care of yourself. As a graduate student and future psychologist, dedicating your career to helping others—whether in clinical work, in research, in education, or elsewhere—it is imperative to recognize and remember that your ability to provide for others as a psychologist is connected to your own well-being and the extent to which you are caring for yourself.

It is very likely that you will experience distress—whether in your personal life, professional life, or both—at some point during your graduate or later professional career. Without the adequate tools to handle such distress, burnout and problems with professional competence are likely to occur over time. Developing awareness and understanding of yourself in relation to risk factors and warning signs in your own life, and incorporating and practicing a self-care regimen are essential components for maintaining personal and professional balance, clinical competence, and ethical standards. Furthermore, consulting with peers and colleagues when unsure of your own wellness and functioning status, and doing the hard work of providing one another with feedback as needed when you have concerns about your colleagues are also essential components of promoting well-functioning within ourselves and throughout the larger professional communities we each are part of.

You face a challenging, uphill battle when it comes to incorporating and practicing self-care within your lifestyle and routine as a student. From the seemingly endless professional and personal demands you juggle and attempt to balance each day, to the academic and training environments that you may work in that frustrate or thwart the promotion of self-care, you will likely be confronted with a number of obstacles to your self-care efforts throughout your graduate school career. Furthermore, new obstacles will continue to present themselves throughout your professional career, making self-care an ongoing effort. Despite this, you cannot afford to ignore or to postpone the integration of self-care and psychological wellness into your personal and professional lifestyles. How you begin to attend to and manage the many challenges and demands you currently face will not only help to address the likely distress experienced at that time, but will build the foundation for how you will respond throughout your career path: a path filled with highs, lows, challenges, and successes.

> *You cannot afford to ignore or to postpone the integration of self-care and psychological wellness into your personal and professional lifestyles.*

Self-care is a lifelong process. As has been discussed throughout this book, you must continue to check in with and amend your self-care ways to tend to the current needs, challenges, and demands of your life. This book is meant to serve as a foundation for gaining awareness and implementing self-care into your life. However, your self-care journey has only just begun. Throughout your remaining time in graduate school, challenges may diminish and new challenges may arise. Personal life experiences and situations may change. As a result, your self-care practices and strategies may require adjustments and modifications as well in order to meet your current needs. This book was also designed for you to return to throughout graduate school and your early professional career for performing self-care tune-ups, assessing your current sources of distress, identifying present warning signs or risk factors, and amending your self-care plans as needed.

As a part of the next generation of psychologists, you hold a considerable degree of responsibility and influence over the future culture of the profession. How you and your graduate student peers choose to value and respond to issues of self-care and psychological wellness in the present will set the stage for the extent to which these values will remain and potentially grow within the profession's culture in the future. Rather than waiting for problems of professional competence or signs of burnout to potentially arise down the road, when you begin to incorporate and attend to self-care today in taking a proactive approach to self-care and psychological wellness, you will be contributing to a foundation and culture of prevention. No such culture of self-care and tending to the well-being of the helper (whether graduate student or psychologist) has previously existed in past generations of mental health professionals.

You have the opportunity to begin to establish a culture of self-care that can have a significant and positive influence for yourself, your current peers, your future colleagues, and your clients alike. In addition to the importance of focusing on our own well-being, we must all remember the role we play as part of a constellation of self-care, a community of colleagues who support, assist, and look out for one another. This is a community that together holds considerable power for protecting and fostering the growth and well-being of present and future psychologists alike.

When you begin to incorporate and attend to self-care today in taking a proactive approach to self-care and psychological wellness, you will be contributing to a foundation and culture of prevention.

Notes

Introduction

1. For example, Barnett & Chesney, 2009; Dearing, Maddux, & Tangney, 2005.
2. Baker, 2003a.
3. Barnett, Baker, Elman, & Shoener, 2007; Barnett, Johnston, & Hillard, 2006.
4. Munsey, 2006.

Chapter 1

1. Barnett et al., 2006, p. 257.
2. Cooper, 2009.
3. Bemak, Epp, & Keys, 1999.
4. Schwartz-Mette, 2009.

Chapter 2

1. Elman & Forrest, 2007, p. 505.
2. Sherman & Thelen, 1998, p. 79.

3. Barnett et al., 2006.
4. Sherman & Thelen, 1998.
5. Guy, Poelstra, & Stark, 1989.
6. Pope, Tabachnick, & Keith-Spiegel, 1987.
7. Huprich & Rudd, 2004.
8. Rosenberg et al., 2005.
9. Boxley et al., 1986; Huprich & Rudd, 2004.
10. Barnett, 2009, p. 797.
11. Knapp & VandeCreek, 2006.
12. Knapp & VandeCreek, 2006.
13. Standard 7.06, APA, 2010.
14. Standard 7.06, APA, 2010.
15. Barnett & Chesney, 2009.
16. Standard 1.04, 1.05, APA, 2010.
17. APA, 2010.
18. APA, 2010, p. 3.
19. APA, 2010, p. 5.
20. APA, 2010, p. 5.
21. APA, 2010, p. 6.
22. APA, 2010, p. 10.
23. APA, 2010.
24. APA, 2010, p. 4.
25. APA, 2010, Standard 2.06.

Chapter 3

1. Vredenburgh, Carlozzi, & Stein, 1999.
2. Kilburg, Nathan, & Thoreson, 1986; Rupert & Morgan, 2005.
3. Brodie & Robinson, 1991.
4. Baker, 2003b, p. 21.
5. Freudenberger, 1975.
6. Skorupa & Agresti, 1993.
7. Maslach & Jackson, 1981.
8. Maslach & Jackson, 1981.
9. Freudenberger, 1975; Maslach & Jackson, 1981.
10. McCarthy & Frieze, 1999.
11. Rupert & Morgan, 2005.
12. Raquepaw & Miller, 1989; Rupert & Morgan, 2005.

13. Acker, 2010; Vredenburgh et al., 1999.

14. Rupert & Morgan, 2005.

15. Rupert & Morgan, 2005.

16. Rupert & Baird, 2004.

17. Rupert & Baird, 2004.

18. Rupert & Baird, 2004.

19. Rupert & Morgan, 2005.

20. Raquepaw & Miller, 1989.

21. Medeiros & Prochaska, 1988.

22. Pipes, Holstein, & Aguirre, 2005.

23. Pipes et al., 2005.

24. Barnett et al., 2007; Barnett et al., 2006.

25. McCarthy & Frieze, 1999.

26. West, Tan, Habermann, Sloan, & Shanafelt, 2009.

Chapter 4

1. McCann & Pearlman, 1990; Figley, 1995.

2. Figley, 1995; McCarthy & Frieze, 1999.

3. McCann & Pearlman, 1990; Newell & MacNeil, 2010.

4. Figley, 1995; Newell & MacNeil, 2010.

5. Figley, 1995, p. 573.

6. Figley, 1995; T. M. O'Halloran & Linton, 2000.

7. Figley, 2002; McCann & Pearlman, 1990; Saakvitne, 2002.

8. M. S. O'Halloran & T. O'Halloran, 2001.

9. Figley, 1995, p. 575.

10. Figley, 1995.

11. Elliott & Guy, 1993.

12. Pope & Feldman-Summers, 1992.

13. Barnett, 2008a; Elliott & Guy, 1993.

14. O'Connor, 2001, p. 346.

15. M. S. O'Halloran & T. O'Halloran, 2001.

16. Pearlman & MacIan, 1995.

17. Pope & Feldman-Summers, 1992.

18. Saakvitne, 2002, p. 447.

19. Figley, 1995.

20. Figley, 1995.

21. M. S. O'Halloran & T. O'Halloran, 2001.

Chapter 5

1. Rupert, Stevanovic, & Hunley, 2009.
2. Barnett et al., 2007; Barnett et al., 2006.
3. Baker, 2003a, p. 10.
4. Pipes, Holstein, & Aguirre, 2005.
5. Pipes et al., 2005.
6. Pipes et al., 2005.
7. Stevanovic & Rupert, 2009.
8. Kilburg et al., 1986.
9. Rupert et al., 2009.
10. Stevanovic & Rupert, 2009.
11. Deacon, Kirkpatrick, Wetchler, & Niedner, 2000.
12. Baker, 2003a, p. 8.
13. Barnett & Sarnel, 2000.
14. Barnett & Sarnel, 2000; M. S. O'Halloran & T. O'Halloran, 2001.
15. Beck, 2010.
16. Sherman & Thelen, 1998.

Chapter 6

1. Atkinson et al., 1994, p. 39.
2. Johnson, 2002, p. 88.
3. APA, 2006; Johnson, 2002.
4. Barnett, 2009; Clark, Harden, & Johnson, 2000; Johnson, 2002.
5. Barnett, 2009.
6. Clark et al., 2000.
7. Clark et al., 2000.
8. Taylor & Neimeyer, 2009.
9. Taylor & Neimeyer, 2009.
10. Norcross & Guy, 2007.
11. Green & Hawley, 2009.
12. Alvarez, Blume, Cervantes, & Thomas, 2009; Russell & Horne, 2009.
13. Clark et al., 2000; Johnson, 2002; Johnson, Koch, Fallow, & Huwe, 2000.
14. Barnett & Cooper, 2009; Schwartz-Mette, 2009.
15. APA, 2006.
16. APA, 2006.
17. APA, 2006.

18. APA, 2006.
19. Johnson, 2002.
20. APA, 2006; Barnett, 2008b.
21. Johnson, 2002, p. 89.
22. APA, 2006.
23. APA, 2006.
24. APA, 2006.

Chapter 7

1. Latham & Locke, 2006.
2. Latham & Locke, 2006.
3. Forsyth, 2007.
4. Covey, 1989.
5. El-Ghoroury & Hillig, 2000.
6. El-Ghoroury & Hillig, 2000.
7. El-Ghoroury & Hillig, 2000.
8. El-Ghoroury & Hillig, 2000.
9. El-Ghoroury & Hillig, 2000.
10. El-Ghoroury & Hillig, 2000.

Chapter 8

1. Norcross & Guy, 2007, p. 204.
2. Baker, 2003a.
3. Baker, 2003a.
4. Norcross & Guy, 2007, p. 14.
5. M. S. O'Halloran & T. O'Halloran, 2001.
6. Norcross & Guy, 2007.
7. Sarnel & Barnett, 1998.
8. Norcross & Guy, 2007, p. 131.
9. Norcross & Guy, 2007; M. S. O'Halloran & T. O'Halloran, 2001.
10. Baker, 2003a.
11. Norcross & Guy, 2007; Stevanovic & Rupert, 2009.
12. Miller & Thoreson, 1999.
13. Baker, 2003a, p. 8.
14. Hill et al., 2000.
15. Case & McMinn, 2001.
16. Mahoney, 1997.
17. Harrison & Westwood, 2009.

18. Zeidan, Johnson, Diamond, David, & Goolkasian, 2010.
19. Barnett & Sarnel, 2000.
20. Barnett & Sarnel, 2000.
21. Mahoney, 1997.
22. Coster & Schwebel, 1997.
23. Cooper, 2009.
24. Holzman, Searight, & Hughes, 1996; Dearing et al., 2005.
25. Holzman et al., 1996.
26. Dearing et al., 2005; Elman & Forrest, 2004.
27. Norcross & Guy, 2007.
28. Barnett & Goncher, 2008.
29. M. S. O'Halloran & T. O'Halloran, 2001.
30. Pope & Tabachnick, 1994.
31. Barnett et al., 2007.
32. Barnett, 2010.
33. Barnett, 2010.
34. Barnett, 2010.
35. Barnett et al., 2007.
36. M. S. O'Halloran & T. O'Halloran, 2001.
37. Green & Hawley, 2009.
38. Adapted from Barnett, Johnston, & Hillard, 2006.

Chapter 9

1. Barnett, 2010.
2. Norcross & Guy, 2007.
3. Norcross & Guy, 2007.
4. Norcross & Guy, 2007.
5. Norcross & Guy, 2007.
6. Baker, 2003a.
7. Barnett, 2009, p. 793.
8. Schwartz-Mette, 2009.
9. Barnett & Cooper, 2009, p. 18.

Chapter 11

1. Johnson, Barnett, Elman, Forrest, & Kaslow, 2012, p. 3.
2. Johnson et al., 2012, p. 3.
3. Barnett, 2008a.

4. Barnett et al., 2007.

5. Dunning, Johnson, Ehrlinger, & Kruger, 2003.

6. Dunning et al., 2003.

7. Hodges, Regehr, & Martin, 2001.

8. Barnett, 2008a, p. 22.

9. For example, Dearing et al., 2005.

10. Jacobs et al., 2011.

11. Barnett & Chesney, 2009; Johnson et al., 2008.

12. Forrest & Elman, 2005.

13. Oliver, Bernstein, Anderson, Blashfield, & Roberts, 2004; Shen-Miller et al., 2011.

14. Barnett et al., 2007, p. 609.

15. Johnson et al., 2012, p. 4.

16. Johnson et al., 2012, p. 26.

17. Johnson, Barnett, Elman Forrest, & Kaslow, 2013.

18. Johnson et al., 2012.

19. Johnson et al., 2013.

20. Johnson et al., 2013.

21. Floyd, Myszka, & Orr, 1998.

22. Oliver et al., 2004; Shen-Miller et al., 2011.

23. Shen-Miller et al., 2011.

24. Mearns & Allen, 1991; Rosenberg et al., 2005.

25. Smith & Moss, 2009, p. 5.

26. Floyd et al., 1998.

27. Oliver et al., 2004.

28. Oliver et al., 2004.

29. Shen-Miller et al., 2011.

30. Barnett, 2008a, p. 868.

31. Barnett, 2008a, p. 868.

32. APA, Board of Professional Affairs Advisory Committee on Colleague Assistance, 2006.

33. Barnett & Hillard, 2001.

34. Johnson et al., 2012, p. 26.

35. Johnson et al., 2013.

Chapter 12

1. Norcross & Guy, 2007, p. 163.

2. Munsey, 2006.

3. American Psychological Association, Commission on Accreditation, 2009.

4. Barnett & Chesney, 2009.

5. Barnett, 2008a, p. 870.

6. Barnett & Chesney, 2009; Barnett & Cooper, 2009.

7. Barnett, 2008a.

8. Coster & Schwebel, 1997.

9. Cooper, 2009.

10. Barnett & Cooper, 2009; Coster & Schwebel, 1997.

11. Bernard & Goodyear, 2013.

12. Norcross & Guy, 2007.

13. Norcross & Guy, 2007, p. 75.

14. Barnett & Cooper, 2009.

15. Barnett & Sarnel, 2000; Coster & Schwebel, 1997.

16. Norcross & Guy, 2007.

17. M. Perry, personal communication, February 13, 2013.

Conclusion

1. El-Ghoroury, 2011.

Resources

The following list of resources, mentioned throughout this handbook, may provide access to additional support and opportunities related to all areas of self-care and psychological wellness discussed herein. This list has been compiled here for quick and easy access for you to use and return to throughout your professional career.

Ethics Codes

American Psychological Association Ethical Principles of Psychologists and Code of Conduct http://www.apa.org/ethics/code/index.aspx

APA Resources

The American Psychological Association of Graduate Students (APAGS) http://www.apa.org/apags
American Psychological Association Division Listings and Resources for Graduate Students http://www.apa.org/about/division/activities/for-students.aspx
APA's Disability Issues Office http://www.apa.org/pi/disability/resources/mentoring/about.aspx

APAGS Committee on LGBT Concerns (APAGS-CLGBTC) http://
www.apa.org/apags/governance/subcommittees/clgbtc-mentor-
ing-program.aspx

APAGS Committee on Ethnic Minority Affairs (APAGS-CEMA)
http://www.apa.org/apags/governance/subcommittees/cema-stra-
tegic-plan.aspx

Specific APA Divisions Mentioned in This Handbook

APA's Division 12 (Clinical Psychology)—www.div12.org

APA's Division 15 (Educational Psychology)—www.apadiv15.org

APA's Division 17 (Counseling Psychology)—www.div17.org

APA's Division 29 (Psychotherapy)—www.divisionofpsychotherapy.
org

APA's Division 38 (Health Psychology)–www.health-psych.org)

APA's Division 39 (Psychoanalysis)—www.apadivisions.org/division-39

APA's Division 40 (Clinical Neuropsychology)—www.div40.org

APA's Division 42 (Psychologists in Independent Practice)—www.
division42.org

APA's Division 43 (Family Psychology)—www.division43apa.org

APA's Division 52 (International Psychology)—www.div52.org

Professional Competence and Colleague Assistance Resources and Programs

American Psychological Association Advisory Committee on
Colleague Assistance (ACCA) http://www.apa.org/practice/lead-
ership/colleague-assistance.aspx

American Psychological Association State, Provincial, and Territorial
Psychological Association Directory http://www.apapracticecen-
tral.org/advocacy/state/associations.aspx

References

Acker, G. M. (2010). The challenges in providing services to clients with mental illness: Managed care, burnout and somatic symptoms among social workers. *Community Mental Health Journal, 46,* 591–600. doi:10.1007/s10597-009-9269-5

Alvarez, A. N., Blume, A. W., Cervantes, J. M., & Thomas, L. R. (2009). Tapping the wisdom tradition: Essential elements to mentoring students of color. *Professional Psychology: Research and Practice, 40,* 181–188. doi:10.1037/a0012256

American Psychological Association. (2010). *Ethical principles of psychologists and code of conduct.* Retrieved from http://www.apa.org/ethics/code/index.aspx

American Psychological Association, Board of Professional Affairs Advisory Committee on Colleague Assistance. (2006). *Advancing colleague assistance in professional psychology.* Washington, DC: Author. Retrieved from http://www.apapracticecentral.org/ce/self-care/colleague-assist-download.pdf

American Psychological Association, Commission on Accreditation. (2009). *Guidelines and principles for accreditation of programs in professional psychology.* Retrieved from http://www.apa.org/ed/accreditation/about/policies/guiding-principles.pdf

Atkinson, D. R., Casas, A., & Neville, H. (1994). Ethnic minority psychologists: Whom they mentor and benefits they derive from the process. *Journal of Multicultural Counseling and Development,* *22,* 37–48. doi:10.1002/j.2161-1912.1994.tb00241.x

Baker, E. K. (2003a). Caring for ourselves as psychologists. The Register Report, *28,* 7–10. Retrieved from http://www.national-register.org/trr.html

Baker, E. K. (2003b). *Caring for ourselves: A psychotherapists' guide to personal and professional well-being.* Washington, DC: American Psychological Association.

Barnett, J. E. (2008a). Impaired professionals: Distress, professional impairment, self-care, and psychological wellness. In M. Herson, & A. M. Gross (Eds.), *Handbook of clinical psychology* (Vol. 1, pp. 857–884). New York, NY: John Wiley & Sons.

Barnett, J. E. (2008b). Mentoring, boundaries, and multiple relationships: Opportunities and challenges. *Mentoring and Tutoring: Partnership in Learning, 16,* 3–16. doi:10.1080/13611260701800900

Barnett, J. E. (2009). The complete practitioner: Still a work in progress. *American Psychologist, 64,* 793–801. doi:10/1037/0003-066x.64.8.793

Barnett, J. E. (2010, May). *Psychological wellness and self-care as an ethical imperative.* Continuing education workshop presented at the Perry Point Veterans Administration Hospital, Perry Point, Maryland.

Barnett, J. E., Baker, E. K., Elman, N. S., & Schoener, G. R. (2007). In pursuit of wellness: The self-care imperative. *Professional Psychology: Research and Practice, 38,* 603–612. doi:10.1037/0735-7028.38.6.603

Barnett, J. E., & Chesney, J. L. (2009). Preventing and addressing impaired professional competence among graduate students in psychology. *Psychotherapy Bulletin, 44,* 22–26. Retrieved from http://www.divisionofpsychotherapy.org/publications/ psychotherapy-bulletin/

Barnett, J. E., & Cooper, N. (2009). Creating a culture of self-care. *Clinical Psychology: Science and Practice, 16,* 16–20. doi:10.1111/j.1468-2850.2009.01138.x

Barnett, J. E., & Goncher, I. (2008). Psychotherapy for the psychotherapist: Optional activity or ethical imperative? *Psychotherapy Bulletin, 43,* 36–40. Retrieved from http://www.divisionofpsycho-therapy.org/publications/psychotherapy-bulletin/

Barnett, J. E., & Hillard, D. (2001). Psychologist distress and impaired professional competence: The availability, nature, and use of colleague assistance programs for psychologists.

Professional Psychology: Research and Practice, 32, 205–210. doi:10.1037/0735-7028.32.2.205

Barnett, J. E., Johnston, L. C., & Hillard, D. (2006). Psychotherapist wellness as an ethical imperative. In L. VandeCreek & J. B. Allen (Eds.), *Innovations in clinical practice: Focus on health and wellness* (pp. 257–271). Sarasota, FL: Professional Resources Press.

Barnett, J. E., & Sarnel, D. (2000). No time for self-care? *42 Online.* The online journal of Psychologists in Independent Practice, a division of the American Psychological Association. Retrieved from http://www.division42.org/StEC /articles/transition/no_time.html

Beck, M. (2010, June 15). Why relaxing is hard work. *The Wall Street Journal.* Retrieved from http://online.wsj.com

Bemak, F., Epp, L. R., & Keys, S. G. (1999). Impaired graduate students: A process model of graduate program monitoring and intervention. *International Journal for the Advancement of Counselling, 21,* 19–30. doi:10.1023/A:1—5387309472

Bernard, J. M., & Goodyear, R. K. (2013). *Fundamentals of clinical supervision* (5th ed). Upper Saddle River, NJ: Pearson Education.

Boxley, R., Drew, C. R., & Rangel, D. M. (1986). Clinical trainee impairment in APA approved internship programs. *The Clinical Psychologist, 39,* 49–52. Retrieved from http://www.div12.org/ clinical-psychologist

Brodie, J., & Robinson, B. (1991). MPA distress/impaired psychologists survey: Overview and results. *Minnesota Psychologist, 41,* 7–10. Retrieved from http://mnpsych.org/displaycommon. cfm?an=1&subarticlenbr=46

Case, P. W., & McMinn, M. R. (2001). Spiritual coping and well-functioning among psychologists. *Journal of Psychology & Theology, 29,* 29–40. Retrieved from http://journals.biola.edu/jpt

Clark, R. A., Harden, S. L., & Johnson, W. B. (2000). Mentor relationships in clinical psychology doctoral training: Results of a national survey. Teaching of Psychology, 27, 262–268. doi:10.1207/ s15328023TOP2704_04

Cooper, N. A. (2009). *A closer look at distress, burnout, stressors, and coping in psychologists today* (Unpublished doctoral dissertation). Loyola University Maryland, Baltimore.

Coster, J. S., & Schwebel, M. (1997). Well-functioning in professional psychologists. *Professional Psychology: Research and Practice, 28,* 5–13. doi:10.1037/0735-7028.28.1.5

Covey, S. R. (1989). *Seven habits of highly effective people: Restoring the character ethic*. New York, NY: Simon and Schuster.

Deacon, S. A., Kirkpatrick, D. R., Wetchler, J. L., & Niedner, D. (2000). Marriage and family therapists' problems and utilization of personal therapy. *The American Journal of Family Therapy, 27,* 73–93. doi:10.1080/019261899262113

Dearing, R. L., Maddux, J. E., & Tangney, J. P. (2005). Predictors of psychological help seeking in clinical and counseling psychology graduate students. *Professional Psychology: Research and Practice, 36,* 323–329. doi:10.1037/0735–7028.36.3.323

Dunning, D., Johnson, K., Ehrlinger, J., & Kruger, J. (2003). Why people fail to recognize their own incompetence. *Current Directions in Psychological Science, 12,* 83–87. doi:10.1111/1467-8721.01235

El-Ghoroury, N. H. (2011, March). Self-care is not just for emergencies. *gradPsych Magazine, 9,* 21. Retrieved from http://www.apa.org/gradpsych/2011/03 /matters.aspx

El-Ghoroury, N. H., & Hillig, J. A. (2000). Cognitive behavioral strategies to improve the graduate school experience: Applying what we learned. *The Behavior Therapist, 23,* 42–44. Retrieved from http://www.abct.org/ Members/?m=mMembers&fa=JournalsPeriodicals#sec3

Elliott, D. M., & Guy, J. D. (1993). Mental health professionals versus non-mental health professionals: Childhood trauma and adult functioning. *Professional Psychology: Research and Practice, 24,* 83–90. doi:10.1037/0735-7028.24.1.83

Elman, N. S., & Forrest, L. (2004). Psychotherapy in the remediation of psychology trainees: Exploratory interviews with training directors. *Professional Psychology: Research and Practice, 35,* 123–130. doi:10.1037/0735-7028.35.2.123

Elman, N. S., & Forrest, L. (2007). From trainee impairment to professional competence problems: Seeking new terminology that facilitates effective action. *Professional Psychology: Research and Practice, 38,* 501–509. doi:10.1037/0735-7028.38.5.501

Figley, C. R. (1995). Systemic traumatization: Secondary traumatic stress disorder in family therapists. In R. Mikesell, D. Lusterman, & S. McDaniel (Eds.), *Integrating family therapy: Handbook of family psychology and systems theory* (pp. 571–581). Washington, DC: American Psychological Association. doi:10.1037/10172-033

Figley, C. R. (2002). Compassion fatigue: Psychotherapists' chronic lack of self care. *Journal of Clinical Psychology* [Special issue on Chronic Illness], *58*, 1433–1441. doi:10.1002/jclp.10090

Floyd, M., Myszka, M. T., & Orr, P. (1998). Licensed psychologists' knowledge and utilization of a state association colleague assistance committee. *Professional Psychology: Research and Practice*, *29*, 594–598. doi:10.1037/0735-7028.29.6.594

Forrest, L., & Elman, N. (2005). Psychotherapy for poorly performing trainees: Are there limits to confidentiality? *Psychotherapy Bulletin*, *40*, 29–37. Retrieved from http://www.divisionofpsychotherapy.org/publications/psychotherapy-bulletin/

Forsyth, P. (2007). *Successful time management* (2nd ed.). London: Kogan Page.

Freudenberger, H. J. (1975). The staff burn-out syndrome in alternative institutions. *Professional Psychology: Research and Practice*, *12*, 73–82. doi:10.1037/h0086411

Green, A. G., & Hawley, G. C. (2009). Early career psychologists: Understanding, engaging, and mentoring tomorrow's leaders. *Professional Psychology: Research and Practice, 40*, 206–212. doi:10.1037/a0012504

Guy, J. D., Poelstra, P. A., & Stark, M. J. (1989). Personal distress and therapeutic effectiveness: National survey of psychologists practicing psychotherapy. *Research and Practice, 20*, 48–50. doi:10.1037/0735-7028.20.1.48

Harrison, R. L., & Westwood, M. J. (2009). Preventing vicarious traumatization of mental health therapists: Identifying protective practices. *Psychotherapy Theory, Research, Practice, Training, 46*, 203–219. doi:10.1037/a0016081

Hill, P. C., Pargament, K. I., Hood, R. W., Jr., McCullough, M. E., Swyers, J. P., Larson, D. B., & Zinnbauer, B. J. (2000). Conceptualizing religion and spirituality: Points of commonality, points of departure. *Journal for the Theory of Social Behaviour, 30*, 51–77. doi:10.1111/1468-5914.00119

Hodges, B., Regehr, G., & Martin, D. (2001). Difficulties in recognizing one's own incompetence: Novice physicians who are unskilled and unaware of it. *Academic Medicine, 76*, S87–S89. doi:10.1097/00001888-200110001-00029

Holzman, L. A., Searight, H. R., Hughes, H. M. (1996). Clinical psychology graduate students and personal psychotherapy: Results of an exploratory survey. *Professional Psychology: Research and Practice, 27*, 98–101. doi:10.1037/0735-7028.27.1.98

Huprich, S. K., & Rudd, M. D. (2004). A national survey of trainee impairment in clinical, counseling, and school psychology doctoral programs and internships. *Journal of Clinical Psychology, 60*, 43–52. doi:10.1002/jclp.10233

Jacobs, S. C., Huprich, S. K., Grus, C. L., Cage, E. A., Elman, N. S., Forrest, L.,…Kaslow, N. J. (2011). Trainees with professional competency problems: Preparing trainers for difficult but necessary conversations. *Training and Education in Professional Psychology, 5*, 175–184. doi:10.1037/a0024656

Johnson, W. B. (2002). The intentional mentor: Strategies and guidelines for the practice of mentoring. *Professional Psychology: Research and Practice, 33*, 88–96. doi:10.1037/0735-7028.33.1.88

Johnson, W. B., Barnett, J. E., Elman, N. S., Forrest, L., & Kaslow, N. J. (2012). The competent community: Toward a vital reformulation of professional ethics. *American Psychologist, 67*, 557–569. doi:10.1037/a0027206

Johnson, W. B., Barnett, J. E., Elman, N. S., Forrest, L., & Kaslow, N. J. (2013, October). The competence constellation model: A communitarian approach to support professional competence. *Professional Psychology: Research and Practice, 44*, 343–354. doi:10.1037/a0033131

Johnson, W. B., Elman, N. S., Forrest, L., Robiner, W. N., Rodolfa, E., & Schaffer, J. B. (2008). Addressing professional competence problems in trainees: Some ethical considerations. *Professional Psychology: Research and Practice, 39*, 589–599. doi:10.1037/a0014264

Johnson, W. B., Koch, C., Fallow, G. O., & Huwe, J. M. (2000). Prevalence of mentoring in clinical versus experimental doctoral programs: Survey findings, implications, and recommendations. *Psychotherapy: Theory, Research, Practice, Training, 37*, 325–334. doi:10.1037/0033-3204.37.4.325

Kilburg, R. R., Nathan, P. E., & Thoreson, R. W. (1986). *Professionals in distress: Issues, syndromes, and solutions in psychology*. Washington, DC: American Psychological Association. doi:10.1037/10056-000

Knapp, S. J., & VandeCreek, L. D. (2006). *Practical ethics for psychologists: A positive approach*. Washington, DC: American Psychological Association.

Latham, G. P., & Locke, E. A. (2006). Enhancing the benefits and over-coming the pitfalls of goal setting. *Organizational Dynamics, 35,* 332–340. doi:10.1016/j.orgdyn.2006.08.008

Mahoney, M. J. (1997). Psychotherapists' personal problems and self-care patterns. *Professional Psychology: Research and Practice, 28,* 14–16. doi:10.1037/0735-7028.28.1.14

Maslach, C., & Jackson, S. E. (1981). The measurement of experi-enced burnout. *Journal of Occupational Behaviour, 2,* 99–113. doi:10.1002/job.4030020205

McCann, I. L., & Pearlman, L. A. (1990). Vicarious traumatiza-tion: A framework for understanding the psychological effects of working with victims. *Journal of Traumatic Stress, 3,* 131–149. doi:10.1007/BF00975140

McCarthy, W. C., & Frieze, I. H. (1999). Negative aspects of psycho-therapy: Client perceptions of psychotherapists' social influence, burnout, and quality of care. *Journal of Social Issues, 55,* 33–50. doi:10.1111/0022-4537.00103

Mearns, J., & Allen, G. J. (1991). Graduate students' experiences in dealing with impaired peers, compared with faculty predic-tions: An exploratory study. *Ethics & Behavior, 1,* 191–202. doi:10.1207/s15327019eb0103_3

Medeiros, M. E., & Prochaska, J. O. (1988). Coping strategies that psychotherapists use in working with stressful clients. *Professional Psychology: Research and Practice, 19,* 112–114. doi:10.1037/0735-7028.19.1.112

Miller, W. R., & Thoreson, C. E. (1999). Spirituality and health. In W. R. Miller (Ed.), *Integrating spirituality into treatment: Resources for practitioners* (pp. 3–18). Washington, DC: American Psychological Association.

Munsey, C. (2006, November). Questions of balance. *Gradpsych, 4*(4). Retrieved from http://www.apa.org/gradpsych/2006/11/cover-bal-ance.aspx

Newell, J. M., & MacNeil, G. A. (2010). Professional burnout, vicarious trauma, secondary traumatic stress, and compassion fatigue: A review of theoretical terms, risk factors, and preventive methods for clinicians and researchers. *Best Practices in Mental Health: An International Journal, 6,* 57–68. Retrieved from http://lyceumbooks.com/MentalHJournal.htm

Norcross, J. C., & Guy, J. D. (2007). *Leaving it at the office: A guide to psychotherapist self-care.* New York, NY: Guilford Press.

O'Connor, M. F. (2001). On the etiology and effective management of professional distress and impairment among psychologists. *Professional Psychology: Research & Practice, 32,* 345–350. doi:10.1037/0735-7028.32.4.345

O'Halloran, M. S., & O'Halloran, T. (2001). Secondary traumatic stress in the classroom: Ameliorating stress in graduate students. *Teaching of Psychology, 28,* 92–97. doi:10.1207/s15328023TOP2802_03

O'Halloran, T. M., & Linton, J. M. (2000). Stress on the job: Self-care resources for counselors. *Journal of Mental Health Counseling, 22,* 354–364. Retrieved from http://www.amhca.org/news/journal.aspx

Oliver, M. N. I., Bernstein, J. H., Anderson, K. G., Blashfield, R. K., & Roberts, M. C. (2004). An exploratory examination of student attitudes toward "impaired" peers in clinical psychology training programs. *Professional Psychology: Research and Practice, 35,* 141–147. doi:10.1037/0735-7028.35.2.141

Pearlman, L. A., & MacIan, P. S. (1995). Vicarious traumatization: An empirical study on the effects of trauma work on trauma therapists. *Professional Psychology: Research and Practice, 26,* 558–565. doi:10.1037/0735-7028.26.6.558

Pipes, R. B., Holstein, J. E., & Aguirre, M. G. (2005). Examining the personal-professional distinction: Ethics codes and the difficulty of drawing a boundary. *American Psychologist, 60,* 325–334. doi:10.1037/0003-066X.60.4.325

Pope, K. S., & Feldman-Summers, S. (1992). National survey of psychologists' sexual and physical abuse history and their evaluation of training and competence in these areas. *Professional Psychology: Research and Practice, 23,* 353–361. doi:10.1037/0735-7028.23.5.353

Pope, K. S., & Tabachnick, B. G. (1994). Therapists as patients: A national survey of psychologists' experiences, problems, and beliefs. *Professional Psychology: Research and Practice, 25,* 247–258. doi:10.1037/0735-7028.25.3.247

Pope, K. S., Tabachnick, B. G., & Keith-Spiegel, P. (1987). Ethics of practice: The beliefs and behaviors of psychologists as psychotherapists. *American Psychologist, 42,* 993–1006. doi:10.1037/0003-066x.42.11.993

Raquepaw, J. M., & Miller, R. S. (1989). Psychotherapist burn-out: A componential analysis. *Professional Psychology: Research and Practice, 20,* 32–36. doi:10.1037/0735-7028.29.1.32

Rosenberg, J. I., Getzelman, M. A., Arcinue, F., & Oren, C. Z. (2005). An exploratory look at students' experiences of prob-lematic peers in academic professional psychology programs. *Professional Psychology: Research and Practice, 36,* 665–673. doi:10.1037/0735-7028.36.6.665

Rupert, P. A., & Baird, K. A. (2004). Managed care and the indepen-dent practice of psychology. *Professional Psychology: Research and Practice, 35,* 185–193. doi:10.1037/0735-7028.35.2.185

Rupert, P. A., & Morgan, D. J. (2005). Work setting and burnout among professional psychologists. *Professional Psychology: Research and Practice, 36,* 544–550. doi:10.1037/0735-7028.36.5.544

Rupert, P. A., Stevanovic, P., & Hunley, H. A. (2009). Work-family conflict and burnout among practicing psychologists. *Professional Psychology: Research and Practice, 40,* 54–61. doi:10.1037/a0012538

Russell, G. M., & Horne, S. G. (2009). Finding equilibrium: Mentoring, sexual orientation, and gender identity. *Professional Psychology: Research and Practice, 40,* 194–200. doi:10.1037/a0011860

Saakvitne, K. M. (2002). Shared trauma—The therapist's increased vulnerability. *Psychoanalytic Dialogues, 12,* 443–449. doi:10.1080/10481881209348678

Sarnel, D., & Barnett, J. E. (1998). Distress and professional impair-ment among psychologists: Implications for professional practice. *The Maryland Psychologist, 44*(2), 17–19. Retrieved from http://www.marylandpsychology.org/psychologists/publications.cfm

Schwartz-Mette, R. A. (2009). Challenges in addressing graduate stu-dent impairment in academic professional psychology programs. *Ethics & Behavior, 19,* 91–102. doi:10.1080/10508420902768973

Shen-Miller, D. S., Grus, C. L., Van Sickle, K. S., Schwartz-Mette, R., Cage, E. A., Elman, N. S., ... Kaslow, N. J. (2011). Trainee's experi-ences with peers having competence problems: A national survey. *Training and Education in Professional Psychology, 5,* 112–121. doi:10.1037/a0023824

Sherman, M. D., & Thelen, M. H. (1998). Distress and professional impaired professional competence among psychologists in clini-cal practice. *Professional Psychology: Research and Practice, 29,* 79–85. doi:10.1037/0735-7028.29.1.79

Skorupa, J., & Agresti, A. A. (1993). Ethical beliefs about burnout and continued professional practice. *Professional Psychology: Research and Practice, 24,* 281–285. doi:10.1037/0735-7028.24.3.281

Smith, P. L., & Moss, S. B. (2009). Psychologist impairment: What is it, how can it be prevented, and what can be done to address it? *Clinical Psychology: Science and Practice, 16,* 1–15. doi:10.1111/j.1468-2850.2009.01137.x

Stevanovic, P., & Rupert, P. A. (2009). Work-family spillover and life satisfaction among professional psychologists. *Professional Psychology: Research and Practice, 40,* 62–68. doi:10.1037/a0012527

Taylor, J. M., & Neimeyer, G. J. (2009). Graduate school mentoring in clinical, counselling, and experimental academic training programs: An exploratory study. *Counselling Psychology Quarterly, 22,* 257–266. doi:10.1080/09515070903157289

Vredenburgh, L. D., Carlozzi, A. F., & Stein, L. B. (1999). Burnout in counseling psychologists: Type of practice setting and pertinent demographics. *Counselling Psychology Quarterly, 12,* 293–302. doi:10.1080/09515079908254099

West, C. P., Tan, A. D., Habermann, T. M., Sloan, J. A., & Shanafelt, T. D. (2009). Association of resident fatigue and distress with perceived medical errors. *The Journal of the American Medical Association, 302,* 1294–1300. doi:10.1001/jama.2009.1389

Zeidan, F., Johnson, S. K., Diamond, B. J., David, Z., & Goolkasian, P. (2010). Mindfulness meditation improves cognition: Evidence of brief mental training. *Consciousness and Cognition, 19,* 597–605. doi:10.1016/j.concog.2010.03.014

About the Authors

Leigh A. Carter, MS, is a doctoral candidate in clinical psychology at Loyola University Maryland. She currently is a pre-doctoral intern at Counseling and Psychological Services in the Department of Student Health at the University of Virginia and will complete a post-doctoral fellowship at University of Delaware's Center for Counseling and Student Development. She is a past board member of the American Psychological Association Advisory Committee on Colleague Assistance and the Maryland Psychological Association for Graduate Students. She has published and presented at professional conferences on the topic of self-care and psychological wellness for graduate students and early career psychologists.

Jeffrey E. Barnett, PsyD, ABPP, is a Professor and Associate Chair in the Department of Psychology at Loyola University Maryland as well as a licensed psychologist in independent practice. He is a Board Certified in Clinical Psychology and in Clinical Child and Adolescent Psychology by the American Board of Professional Psychology, and he is a Distinguished Practitioner in the National Academies of Practice. He has published extensively and does training on self-care, promoting psychological wellness, burnout prevention, ethics, and professional practice issues.

Index